THE INTERPRETATION OF DREAMS

FREUD'S
THEORIES REVISITED

TWAYNE'S MASTERWORK STUDIES
Robert Lecker, General Editor

THE
INTERPRETATION
OF DREAMS
FREUD'S
THEORIES REVISITED

Laurence M. Porter

Twayne Publishers • Boston
A Division of G.K. Hall & Co.

The Interpretation of Dreams: Freud's Theories Revisited

Laurence M. Porter

Twayne's Masterwork Studies No. 9

Copyright 1987 by G.K. Hall & Co.
All rights reserved.
Published by Twayne Publishers
A Division of G.K. Hall & Co.
70 Lincoln Street
Boston, Massachusetts 02111

Copyediting supervised by Lewis DeSimone
Book production by Janet Zietowski

Typeset in 10/14 Sabon with Caslon 540 Display type
by Compset, Inc. of Beverly, Massachusetts

Printed on permanent/durable acid-free paper
and bound in the United States of America

Library of Congress Cataloging-in-Publication Data

Porter, Laurence M., 1936–
    The interpretation of dreams.

    (Twayne's masterwork studies ; no. 9)
    Bibliography: p.
    Includes index.
    1. Freud, Sigmund, 1856–1939. Traumdeutung. 2. Dreams.
3. Psychoanalysis. I. Title. II. Series.
BF1078.F73P67   1987   154.6′3   87-11940
ISBN 0-8057-7971-X (alk. paper)
ISBN 0-8057-8009-2 (pbk. : alk. paper)

For Laurel,
who made my dreams come true

Contents

The Interpretation of Dreams

Note on References and Acknowledgments

The authoritative edition of Freud's works in English is *The Standard Edition of the Complete Works of Sigmund Freud,* edited and translated by James Strachey (London: Hogarth, 1953–74), 24 vols., traditionally referred to as *SE.* Each volume has excellent introductions tracing the development of Freud's thought, and a valuable index to concepts discussed. Volumes 4 and 5 contain *The Interpretation of Dreams.* This text includes all the additions and revisions that Freud made during his lifetime, through the 8th German edition of 1930. Freud usually let earlier remarks stand alongside later ones, so as to reveal the evolution of his thought. The same Strachey text was later published by Basic Books in New York, and finally brought out in an inexpensive paperback edition entitled *The Interpretation of Dreams* (New York: Avon, 1980 [1965]). This paperback is the text referred to by page number alone throughout the present volume. Citations from all of Freud's other works are from the *SE.*

Many people help to make a book. I am indebted to the generosity of Professor Harold Zepelin of the Department of Psychology at Oakland University, who brought me up to date on sleep and dream research; and to the patience and expertise of four kind friends and colleagues who read the entire manuscript, offering many valuable suggestions for improvement: Laurel Porter, ACSW, a clinical social worker with Child and Family Services in Lansing, Michigan; and Professors Gilbert Chaitin of the Department of French and Italian at the University of Indiana; Herbert Josephs of the Department of Romance and Classical Languages at Michigan State University; and Colin

Martindale of the Department of Psychology at the University of Maine at Orono. They will recognize their influence throughout. They rescued me from many blunders and obscurities. To Dr. Edward Gibeau, psychotherapist and president of the Lansing chapter of the Michigan Society for Psychoanalytic Psychology, I am grateful for years of encouragement and for his enlightening conversations about psychoanalysis and psychoanalytic theory, as well as for his inspirational enthusiasm and commitment. The Interlibrary Loan Service of Michigan State University did yeoman service in providing articles from foreign periodicals. I would also like to thank the Department of Romance and Classical Languages, the Office of the Dean of the College of Arts and Letters, and the All-University Research Fund of Michigan State University for providing funds to copy research materials and to type the manuscript. Our department chairperson, George Mansour, has greatly facilitated the completion of this project through his active, unfailing encouragement of scholarly research. Once again, as for over twenty years of our association, Joy Walker did impeccable work in typing the final draft. To Anne Jones of Twayne Publishers I am thankful for her conceiving a series that is eminently rewarding to write for. Above all, I am obligated to Professor Robert Lecker of the Department of English at McGill University. As series editor he understood better than I what book I would find most interesting and exciting to write; his vision and his strong, consistent support literally made it possible.

Portrait of Freud by his children, ca. 1907. *Courtesy of the Prints and Photographs Division, The Library of Congress, and of Sigmund Freud Copyrights, Colchester, England.*

Chronology: Sigmund Freud's Life and Works

1856	Freud is born in Freiburg, Austria (now in Czechoslovakia). In 1859 the family moves to Leipzig and in 1860 to Vienna, where he remains for the next seventy-eight years.
1873–1881	Owing to his many interests, Freud spends three years longer than average as a medical student. To help his studies, his adoring family gives him their only oil lamp, a private bedroom (seven people share the other three), and serves him dinners in his room. During his last four years he serves an apprenticeship as a neurologist with the famous Ernst Brücke, laying the groundwork for the modern unitary theory of neurons (nerve cells).
1881–1886	Freud moves into the Vienna General Hospital and trains as a resident in surgery, internal medicine, psychiatry, ophthalmology, and dermatology. He discovers the medical uses of cocaine as a local anesthetic and antidepressant. With horror, he then learns the dangers of the drug when some of his patients become addicts and one dies of an overdose.
1882–1886	Freud's courtship of Martha Bernays (born 1861) produces a thousand eloquent love letters.
1885–1886	Freud receives a traveling fellowship to study for four months with Charcot, the most famous neurologist of his time, in his clinic in Paris. Charcot's lectures on mental illness are a revelation to Freud. He changes careers, becoming a psychiatrist.
1886	Freud marries Martha and opens a private practice in Vienna. Three sons and three daughters are born to the Freuds between 1887 and 1895; the youngest, Anna, will become a famous psychoanalyst. For the next ten years, Freud does important research on hysteria with Josef Breuer.
1889	Freud spends several weeks during the summer watching the famous hypnotherapist Hippolyte Bernheim at work in Nancy,

Freud's engagement picture with Martha Bernays, 1886. *Courtesy of Mary Evans / Sigmund Freud Copyrights.*

France. Freud even brings along a patient of his in hopes that Bernheim might cure her. "I received the profoundest impression of the possibility that there could be powerful mental processes which nevertheless remained hidden from the consciousness of man" (cited by Jones, 1:238).

1892–1895   Freud stops using hypnotic suggestion to treat hysteria when he discovers that his patients' improvement is not lasting. He identifies the decisive roles of repressed sexuality and of infantile thinking in neurosis. He gradually develops the "talking cure" that becomes the basis of psychoanalytic technique whereby patients engage in free association that relieves the tension caused by unconscious conflicts emerging into awareness.

1887–1902   A close friendship with the Berlin nose specialist Wilhelm Fliess produces a series of letters essential for understanding how Freud developed psychoanalysis. From Fliess, Freud gets the key ideas of sublimation, the latency period, and the fundamental bisexuality of all human beings.

1896   Freud's father dies.

1897–1900   Freud begins a profound self-analysis as he attempts to overcome his mood swings, tachycardia (surges of rapid heartbeat), self-diagnosed latent homosexuality, fear of train travel, and fear of death. For the rest of his life he will devote half an hour a day to self-analysis.

1899   Publication of Freud's masterpiece *The Interpretation of Dreams* (postdated 1900) in November. Freud feels that his book is either attacked or ignored, but in fact it receives prompt, respectful, and widespread attention.

1902   Freud's psychiatric practice expands greatly once he is named professor at the university. He becomes comfortably well-off. He has no formal duties, but delivers two unpaid lectures a week most years up until World War I. In the fall, Freud starts a Wednesday discussion group with the psychiatrists Adler, Kahane, Reitler, and Stekel. This grows into the Vienna Psycho-Analytical Society with twenty-two members and a substantial library destroyed by the Nazis in 1938. Otto Rank (1906), Sandor Ferenczi (1908) and Hanns Sachs (1910) join. Famous guests include Karl Abraham, A. A. Brill, Ernest Jones, and Carl Gustav Jung.

1904   Freud's *Psychopathology of Everyday Life* explains that slips of the tongue and pen, forgetting, mislaying things, and other unintended actions—like dreams—derive from repressed wishes.

1905   The "Fragment of an Analysis of a Case of Hysteria" (the "Dora" case) illustrates the use of dream interpretation in psychoanalysis. (Over the past twenty years, feminists have found Freud's handling of this case highly controversial.) *Three Essays on the Theory of Sexuality* shocks many by asserting that infants have sexual desires and that the first objects of these desires are the parents. For the next ten years, Freud and his followers are attacked as dangerous perverts who advocate abandoning all civilized restraints.

1907   *Delusion and Dreams in Jensen's "Gradiva,"* a masterful, pioneering psychoanalytic study of a literary work. International recognition of Freud begins. He makes contact with the Hungarian Sandor Ferenczi, who becomes his closest friend and collaborator, and with Swiss analysts from Zurich. One of them, Max Eitingon, undergoes the first recorded training analysis with Freud in 1907 and 1909. Another Swiss, Carl Gustav Jung, is designated Freud's "son and heir" when Freud names him president of the International Association of Psychoanalysis at its founding in 1910. Two years later, Jung starts attacking Freud in public, and breaks with him in 1913.

1908   The First International Psychoanalytic Congress meets in Salzburg.

1909   Freud gives five lectures at Clark University in Worcester, Massachusetts, and receives an honorary doctorate there. The great philosopher and psychologist William James tells him that "the future of psychology belongs to your work." But Freud dislikes America, being bothered by its peculiar accents, its informality, and its materialism. He calls the country "a gigantic mistake."

1910   "Leonardo da Vinci and a Memory of His Childhood," the first real psychobiography.

1911   "Psychoanalytical Notes on an Autobiographical Account of a Case of Paranoia" (the Schreber case). In the important final chapter Freud links paranoia to repressed homosexuality and also discusses the mechanisms of psychic repression. "Formulations on the Two Principles of Mental Functioning," a classic, influential essay, distinguishes a "pleasure principle" and a "reality principle" contending in the psyche. Break with Stekel and with Adler, who are jealous of Jung. Ernest Jones founds the American Psychoanalytical Association.

1912   Freud founds the psychoanalytic journal *Imago.*

1913   *Totem and Taboo* links the origins of religion to relations with the parents.

Chronology: Sigmund Freud's Life and Works

1916–1917   *Introductory Lectures on Psycho-Analysis,* the most widely used exposition of Freudian theory. Lectures 5–15 treat dreams. "Mourning and Melancholia," still one of the best accounts of clinical depression. "Notes on a Case of Obsessional Neurosis" (the "Rat Man") explains that such patients are terrified that their wishes may come true; they ward them off with superstitious rituals.

1918   "From the History of an Infantile Neurosis" (the "Wolf Man") asserts the importance of the primal scene (parental intercourse witnessed or overheard by infants and small children) in neurotics' fantasy life.

1918–1920   The end of the war and its aftermath inflict severe hardship on Freud: little food, light, or heat, and a catastrophic inflation that drains away all his savings.

1919   Freud founds the Internationaler Psychoanalytischer Verlag (press); over the next twenty years it publishes 150 books and 5 journals, including Freud's complete works in German. To support the enterprise, Freud declines all royalties.

1920   *The International Journal of Psychoanalysis* (still appearing) is founded. Freud's financial difficulties are alleviated by a flood of aspiring analysts coming from England and America to be trained. He sometimes sees ten a day.

1923   Freud, who for years smoked up to twenty cigars a day when he could get them, is found to have cancer of the mouth. He undergoes the first of thirty-three operations, and drastic radium treatments, temporarily successful, but he remains in pain most of the rest of his life. *The Ego and the Id* presents important speculations about a "superego" springing from a repressed Oedipus complex and from identification with the parents' own superegos. *Beyond the Pleasure Principle* speculates about a "death instinct" based on an organism's desire to revert to a state of total tranquility. This notion has never been widely accepted.

1924   Rank breaks with Freud.

1926   "Inhibitions, Symptoms and Anxiety," Freud's major clinical contribution after World War I, develops the concept of psychic defenses and their origins in the neuroses. The cancer returns. Freud loses the entire right side of his upper jaw and palate. From this point on he must wear a prosthesis to separate his mouth from his nasal cavity to make speaking and eating possible. Despite frequent alterations, the device remains most uncomfortable. Therefore American psychoanalysts, most of whom train with Freud after this date, get the image of a therapist who only grunts and nods; they perpetuate this tradition. Freud's true style, however, involved frequent intervention and interpretation, and ordinary conversation as well, as his published case histories show.

1926–1927   Freud fights for the right of lay people (nonphysicians) to perform psychoanalysis; the Americans refuse to accept this under any circumstances.

1929   Break with Ferenczi.

1930   *Civilization and Its Discontents* explains that civilized restraints and psychic discomfort are inseparable. Freud receives the Goethe Prize for excellence in prose style.

1933   In Berlin, Hitler seizes and burns psychoanalytic books.

1934   Hitler outlaws psychoanalysis in Germany, expels all Jewish analysts, and bans Jews from all scientific bodies.

1938   In March, the Nazis take over Austria. They twice search Freud's apartment and briefly detain his daughter Anna. Both Mussolini and Franklin D. Roosevelt intervene. Fearing a worldwide scandal, the Nazis allow Freud and his family to leave for London after extorting a large sum of money from them.

1939   The cancer flares up again in February; it has become inoperable. Freud dies 23 September.

1940   The posthumous "Outline of Psycho-Analysis" remains the best general theoretical statement on psychoanalysis.

1

Historical Context

At the end of the nineteenth century, Freud's Austria seemed a secure and tranquil place. An ambitious urban development program had made the capital, Vienna, into one of the world's most charming, imposing cities. The Industrial Revolution had spread prosperity and modern comforts throughout much of Europe. And the Austrian monarchy had endured for nearly one thousand years. War seemed unlikely. After suffering military setbacks in Prussia and in Italy at mid-century, Austria had consolidated its power base in Central Europe by forming a Dual Monarchy with Hungary in 1867 and by acquiring the right to administer the former Turkish provinces of Bosnia and Herzegovina as protectorates. These were to be annexed by Austria-Hungary after the Young Turks' revolution in 1908.

But dark clouds were gathering on the horizon. Within Austria, the rabble-rousing, anti-Semitic New Right party of Christian Socialists led by Karl Lueger captured the city government of liberal Vienna in 1895. The parliament of the Dual Monarchies of Austria and Hungary was paralyzed by factionalism during the late 1890s. On the international scene, Austria had missed out on the wave of European imperialist expansion into Africa and Asia that culminated in

1880–95. And in Europe, the growing power and aggressiveness of Prussia (later the major member state of modern Germany) under Bismarck foreshadowed the devastation of World War I ultimately followed by Hitler's annexation of Austria in 1938.

It is difficult for an American, and especially for one living a century after Freud, to imagine what a class-conscious, rigidly structured society he lived in. The vast majority of people belonged to a mass of laborers, peasants, and domestic servants who often could barely read and write and who could never hope to become financially independent or advance to a better job. Once Freud became established he had three servants in his own household. They were taken for granted; he never mentioned them in writing; and at least once, off the record, he admitted that he despised persons from the "lower class." But Freud was a victim of the class system as well as a beneficiary. In his childhood he had dreamed of a political or military career. But political and military leaders came from the ranks of the hereditary aristocracy. Few bourgeois and hardly any Jews could aspire to such posts. So Freud shelved his ambitions to become a public figure, and decided to seek fame as a scientist. Even there he faced severe constraints. Despite his outstanding publications in pharmacology and in neurology he could not become a research scientist because the universities where such scientists worked paid too little to support them, and Freud did not have an independent income. Finally, as a medical practitioner in status-conscious Vienna, Freud needed an impressive university title to attract patients and to command adequate fees. Despite his international reputation, he had to wait seventeen years rather than the normal eight for the all-important promotion from Privat-Dozent (Lecturer) to Professor Extraordinarius (Associate Professor). Was the delay caused by bureaucratic inertia, by Freud's technical lack of qualifications (he had been a lecturer in neurology, not in psychiatry), or by anti-Semitism—or a combination of these? This hotly debated question remains unresolved.[1]

The bourgeoisie, Freud's social class, had one thing in common with the aristocracy: an elitist education concentrating heavily on languages and literature. Everyone who finished secondary school—a small percentage compared to today—had taken seven years of Latin and studied two or three other languages. Freud, who had a gift for languages and for writing, was fluent in English and French. He had a fair command of Spanish and Italian as well. He knew Greek mythology. He loved literature and read widely, particularly in Shakespeare and in nineteenth-century German, Swiss, and Austrian drama and fiction. His own writings are full of literary allusions. He modeled his style on that of Goethe, the greatest German writer of all time. His favorite book was Goethe's *Faust*. He quotes from it frequently, confident that his readers will recognize not only the quotations but also their context. As a result of this shared cultural heritage among educated people, the "two cultures"—scientific and humanistic—were much closer than they are today. Medicine was not exclusively scientific and technical. Some traces of that tradition remain in Europe today. If you go to a doctor there, you may hear a philosophical discussion about the nature of illness and related questions during part of your consultation. Freud himself saw psychoanalysis as an interdisciplinary rather than a medical specialty.

Women of all classes, however, were largely excluded from these educational advantages. If they were well-to-do, they received some training in language, literature, and the arts in order to make them more polished social companions; but they were expected to be only housewives and mothers. In 1900 women were barred from most professions. If they did not want marriage and children, they had little choice. A few middle-class women, married or not, unconsciously rebelled against their femininity and its prescribed roles by retreating into a "sick role" of psychosomatic illness that excused them from fulfilling what were then considered the normal duties of womanhood. At the time, a catch-all label for such illness was "hysteria," and many of Freud's early patients were "hysterics."

At the end of the nineteenth century, the treatment of choice for hysterics was hypnosis. Freud learned hypnosis with the great Jean Martin Charcot in Paris and then used it in collaboration with Josef Breuer. The essentials of the doctor-patient relationship in psychoanalysis as Freud developed it were to grow out of hypnotherapy. Both techniques start by building a relationship of trust. This allows the patient eventually either to enter a trance or to associate freely, or both, reporting anything that comes to mind. Both processes bring hidden memories to light and involve regression to childhood experiences. The patient's growing dependence on the doctor initially aids the therapy, but before it ends, the patient's independence must be restored. The great advantage of psychoanalysis over hypnotism is that the active participation of the patient lays the groundwork for self-knowledge and for long-term personality change, rather than being limited to the temporary alleviation of symptoms. That is why Freud abandoned hypnosis.[2]

Freud did not invent psychoanalytic theory from nothing. The influences of Darwin, Nietzsche, and Schopenhauer were important in forming his concepts of the Oedipus complex, the superego, and a dynamic unconscious in conflict with the conscious self. The work of Gustav Theodor Fechner (1801–87) inspired Freud's notions of mental energy, the repetition compulsion, superimposed layers of psychic contents from different periods of life, and the pleasure principle (the organism's instinctive attempt to maintain a constant but not excessive level of stimulation). His contemporary Pierre Janet (1859–1947) gave him the idea of neurotic complexes (which Janet called "unconscious fixed ideas") and their possible cure through catharsis (purging), which recovered and reenacted the unconscious traumatic memory, followed by "working through"—assimilating the experience to rational awareness gradually without being overwhelmed by it. Janet also anticipated Freud in discussing repression ("the narrowing of consciousness"—although he saw it as a passive dissociation from rather than an active banishing of threatening thoughts), the reality principle, free association ("automatic talking"), and transference (the patient's projections of unconscious fantasies on the doctor, who is thus identified with a significant other in the patient's earlier life). In short, Freud's concept of psychotherapy seems consistently modeled on Janet's.[3] But Freud achieved lasting international fame and Janet did not. First, Janet shifted his investigations from the unconscious to "psychological tension."[4] Second, Freud discovered an explanation for repression and Janet did not. And finally, Janet spoke better than he wrote, whereas Freud was both a great writer and a prolific one whose graceful prose and skillful arguments commanded widespread attention.

Keenly sensitive to anti-Semitism, criticism, and attacks, Freud saw himself as an isolated, embattled figure surrounded by a small elite of loyal followers as he unmasked hypocrisy and self-deception. It is true that the medical establishment, whose approval Freud wanted most, never gave him unconditional acceptance, and that several of his disciples rebelled. But from the 1920s on, his has unquestionably been the predominant influence on psychology, literature, and the history of ideas. In twentieth-century thought, only Karl Marx has been of comparable importance.

2

The Importance of the Work

Freud's greatest contribution to the study of dreams was to demonstrate that they reveal something important about the dreamer. Before the Freudian era opinion had been polarized. From the mid-eighteenth century on, scientists and Enlightenment philosophers had believed that dreams revealed nothing important whatsoever. They were held to be the accidental products of an unoccupied mind drifting and generating random combinations of ideas during sleep. At the other extreme, the visionary writers and philosophers of the late eighteenth century and romanticism had claimed that dreams were the vehicles of a transcendent religious truth, doorways to the supernatural.[1] Freud refuted these notions by proving that dreams were both purposeful and personal. He found their source in repressed childhood experiences. He thought that dreams could ultimately be traced to unresolved conflicts springing from the child's problematic relations with its parents. One of the two major differences between psychology in general and psychoanalysis in particular is that the latter insists we cannot fully understand our emotional problems without first understanding our childhood.

The other major differen is that psychoanalysis always

conceives of the conscious, adapting, coping part of the mind as in conflict with another part. More vividly and richly than any previous thinker, Freud depicted the mind as a battleground between past and present, impulse and inhibition, the unconscious and consciousness. He assumed that all human behavior has a motivational cause, and that involuntary behavior always is ambivalent because it is motivated by these two sets of opposing forces. He believed the only cure for mental illness was to bring the unconscious to light. So he tried to gain access to it by examining the areas where it showed through in everyday life: in the involuntary behavior of dreams, mistakes, and forgetting. His major, most lasting achievement was a subtle analysis of the dynamic relationship between trauma (a damaging experience—from the Greek word for "wound") and neurotic symptom, concealed motive and overt actions, the latent and the manifest content of the dream.

Freud's ideas concerning dreams and psychoanalysis became widely accepted because he was one of the greatest writers in the history of the German language. He possessed an enormously rich yet unaffected vocabulary and an unusually distinctive style, recognizable at a glance. He had a gift for presenting complex arguments simply. He had an urbane grace, an unfailing instinct for the most expressive word, and an uncanny knack for predicting what objections would arise in the reader's mind at any point in his arguments (Jones, 2:209–10 and 410). These qualities gave his ideas far more impact than they would otherwise have had.

Finally, Freud's use of dreams in therapy marked a major advance toward understanding the psyche. His asking patients for free associations to the details of their dreams remains a basic technique of psychoanalysis, even among those such as Jungians whose views on human personality are radically different. More generally, Freud's discoveries have made us keenly aware of how influential our relationships to significant others in childhood are—not only by imprinting the future adult with models for all her or his later relationships, but also in forming our entire culture and society.[2]

By examining the vital junction point of mind and body, the

intersection of impulse and inhibition, Freud destroyed rigid, artificial divisions between sick and healthy, conscious and unconscious, will and accident, psychology and psychiatry, philosophy and medicine. Since the mid-twenties Freud's influence has spread far beyond the medical profession. Between the two world wars, the French surrealists systematically applied Freudian concepts to a sustained investigation of the unconscious. They recorded dreams and experimented extensively with trances, automatic writing, and free association in an attempt to discover uncharted territory for the imagination. Film is probably the greatest artistic achievement of the twentieth century, and beginning with the surrealists, great filmmakers like Cocteau, Buñuel, Fellini, and Bergman have used dream sequences in their work, with many allusions to the Freudian concept of dreams in both content and in structure. And in myriad novels, films, and television dramas today, the psychoanalytic setting itself appears everywhere from Mickey Spillane to Woody Allen to *The White Hotel*. Imagine a world without Freud, and you have a world where mental illness would be treated either by priests or by injections. Insofar as it goes beyond kindness and common sense, the healing art of clinical social workers, psychologists, psychiatrists, and counselors grew mainly out of Freudian psychoanalysis.[3]

The "Committee" and Sigmund Freud, Berlin, 1922. From left to right: standing—
Rank, Abraham, Eitingon, Jones; sitting—Freud, Ferenzci, Sachs. *Courtesy of Mary
Evans / Sigmund Freud Copyrights.*

3

Critical Reception

In his preface to the first edition of *The Interpretation of Dreams* Freud explained that he wanted to discuss dreams not only because they were important in and of themselves, but also because they were a prime example of "abnormal psychic phenomena." By that he meant involuntary, unintentional mental activity. He thought that if you could understand how dreams originate, you would also understand how phobias, obsessions, and delusions do, because the mind works the same way in creating the latter as in creating the former. So understanding dream formation would ultimately lead to understanding and being able to cure mental illness. Freud then explained the difficulties he faced in finding dreams suitable for discussion. Dreams already published by others would not do because they lacked the dreamers' associations to each detail of the dream narrative. Without these associations the personal meaning of the dreams remains obscure. Dreams from his own patients were excessively complicated and distorted by neurotic symptoms, he claimed. Freud wanted to start building his dream theory on the basis of commonplace, everyday dreams that illustrated universal human traits. The only remaining source was Freud's own dreams. These would reveal more of his intimate feelings than he wanted to make public. He resigned himself to using them anyway, but asked the reader's indulgence for the defensive "omissions and substitutions" that he imposed on his dreams for discretion's sake.[1]

So Freud intended to use dreams to explain neurosis. His preface unwittingly points to two major conceptual flaws in the execution of his project. He planned to explain neurotic symptoms as analogous to dreams, by extrapolating from dream theory. But as his book unfolds, it instead extrapolates from his theories of neurosis in order to explain dreams. Second, he actually reports patients' dreams as well as his own. Presumably, he selected from among their dreams—and then from among their associations to the chosen dreams—in order to avoid the undesirable complications of neurotic thought. By doing this, and by suppressing the embarrassing personal and sexual details in his own associations, Freud was turning away from the very elements of the dreams that would have helped him to explore their connections to psychopathology. The result is that none of the dream interpretations in the book illustrates his major thesis: dreams are disguised expressions of repressed wishes rooted in infantile sexual reactions to the parents. Freud's theoretical argument in *The Interpretation of Dreams* becomes gravely weakened because he never traces the latent dream thoughts back to such infantile material.

Freud's preface to the second, 1908 edition acknowledges a personal as well as a theoretical theme: in retrospect he sees the work as a portion of the self-analysis precipitated by his father's death in 1896. Within the text, Freud never made this theme fully explicit; he never summed up and evaluated his overall psychological development. For the last twenty years, critics have tried to do so for him, reading *The Interpretation of Dreams* as a disguised confessional autobiography (Hyman) or interpreting Freud's individual dreams more thoroughly than he himself had done (Elms, Grinstein, Swan) (Ellenberger, 451).[2] Since Freud occasionally masked his own dreams by presenting them as his patients', some sensation-seeking critics have speculated that other "patients'" dreams were also Freud's. This device has allowed them to spin scandalous, but unsubstantiated, accounts of Freud's life.

These historical romances, however, do not throw light on dream theory.[3]

The 1911 preface to the third edition marks a retreat from the personal to the general. There Freud explains that his increasing clinical experience plus the influence of Wilhelm Stekel led him to recognize that universal symbolism is more important in dreams than he had previously believed when he thought that the dreamer's associations to each image in the dream could decode it completely. Soon after, Freud broke with Stekel, but he continued to add examples of universal symbolism to the following editions of *The Interpretation of Dreams*. Freud often vehemently protested that symbolic interpretation could never be anything more than a secondary, supplementary technique: the dreamer's associations were essential. And he made it clear that not all symbols are sexual: he emphasizes sexual symbols only because sexuality is what we are most reluctant to recognize in neurotic illness—above all else, such illness is an inability to love. Nevertheless, misled by the ample space Freud ended up devoting to symbolism, many psychologists and critics, particularly in the 1940s and 1950s, dedicated themselves to compiling tedious catalogues of "Freudian [i.e., sexual] symbolism" in dreams, art, and literature.

Freud tried to strengthen the theoretical connections between dreams and neurosis in 1916–17 when he wrote chapters 5–15 of the masterful *Introductory Lectures on Psycho-Analysis* as a simplified, updated version of *The Interpretation of Dreams* (see his 1918 preface to the latter). But he never considered that the earlier work had been superseded. In fact, he always regarded it as his masterpiece. In 1931 he prefaced the third English edition by saying that his views regarding dreams remained "essentially unaltered." He said that the book presented "the most valuable of all the discoveries it has been my good fortune to make," and added: "Insight such as this falls to one's lot but once in a lifetime" (xxxii).

Legend has it that *The Interpretation of Dreams* was almost totally neglected when it appeared, or else unfairly attacked by Freud's medical colleagues; only after a number of years was it appreciated by a widening circle of cultivated general readers who did not share the scientists' prejudices. This legend was started by Freud himself (see 1908 preface, xxv) and perpetuated in Ernest Jones's biography. The truth is nearly the opposite. Freud enjoyed renown in medical circles before, during, and after 1899. *The Interpretation of Dreams* was widely, favorably reviewed in prestigious journals, although only 351 copies sold in the first six years: Freud enjoyed a critical, but not a popular success at first.

He attracted attention because no serious work on the interpretation of dreams had appeared since K. A. Scherner's in 1861, and he was further helped by the immediate international success of Theodore Flournoy's classic *From India to Planet Mars,* which also appeared in 1899. Flournoy described his five-year investigation of the Geneva medium Catherine Müller, who claimed to have the gift of clairvoyance and the ability to recall former lives including one on Mars, whose "language" she spoke and wrote fluently when in a trance. Flournoy explained how her subconscious imagination drew upon forgotten childhood experiences (as Freud's dreams did also) to fabricate her fictional past lives and her invented language. Beneath all her fantasy roles, he identified the fundamental unity of her personality. After reading Flournoy, people who wanted to know more about the relationships between childhood and fantasies turned to Freud.

Freud had already been singled out as one of the world's leading authorities on hysteria at the International Psychological Congress in 1896. His biography appeared in a medical *Who's Who* in 1901. For the remainder of his career, so far as we know, he never had a book or article rejected by a publisher (Ellenberger, 453–55). And after its slow start, *The Interpretation of Dreams* went through seven more German editions between 1909 and 1930, with English editions in 1913, 1915, and 1932. In 1900 the book was promptly and favorably reviewed by well-known authors in three Viennese newspapers and a Berlin magazine. It received at least eleven additional reviews in journals that included highly regarded periodicals in medicine, psychiatry, and psychology. The international bibliographies in psychology *and* philosophy listed Freud's work within months; the leading French philosopher of the day, Henri Bergson, quoted it in a lecture early in 1901, and Jung mentioned it in his 1902 dissertation (Ellenberger, 783–84).[4]

Only one commentator took issue with Freud's basic hypothesis that dreams fulfill wishes. Those who wanted to express reservations because Freud's theories had not been tested by controlled scientific experimentation did so only indirectly by praising him for being "ingenious" (*geistvoll* or *geistreich*). The brilliant pathologist Otto Lubarsch (1860–1933) called Freud's conception of dreams "extraordinarily fruitful"—as indeed it proved to be—and added that Freud's work had helped him understand many of his own dreams for the first time. Others praised him as the "Columbus of dream research" and "the first to have established the laws that govern dreams." Nobody disagreed that childhood experiences and impressions were woven into dreams along with current preoccupations. Every reviewer accepted the notion that dreams are "the guardians of sleep," forestalling awakening by weaving external and internal physical stimuli into the fabric of the dream images. Everyone likewise allowed that unconscious mental processes exist in every person and that these regularly affect our conscious thoughts and actions. Only Wilhelm Weygandt attacked as shocking and extreme the notion of an Oedipus complex: that a child could be sexually attracted to the parent of the opposite sex and wish to get rid of the rival parent of the same sex. Most reviewers shied away from the topic of infantile sexuality by not mentioning it.[5]

But the idea that the early twentieth century was a prudish, "Victorian" age unable to tolerate any discussion of sexuality is a myth. In fact, like the twenties and late sixties, it was a period of relative sexual license, with "Leagues of Free Love" (reminiscent of the fantasy of unlimited sex in "hippie communes") and hot debates about contraception. Besides, *The Interpretation of Dreams* did not clearly present Freud's most radical theories of sexuality. Only some years later did his concept of the "Oedipus complex" emerge in sharp outline. In the years just before World War I this aroused horror in some opponents—as did Freud's recognition that the anus could be an erogenous zone. By 1910 psychoanalysis had become an organized international movement and Freud's detractors feared that it was undermining public morals by advocating the infantile sexual tendencies that it was actually trying to help neurotics outgrow.

With such an overwhelmingly favorable response by reviewers, one might wonder why Freud was dissatisfied. The answers seem to be that his masterpiece did not sell well for a number of years; that he was keenly sensitive to any hint of criticism; but above all, that he had hoped for a wider response from the scientific community. He was relatively unaware of or indifferent to the nonprofessional responses to his work—he welcomed them, but he passed up many opportunities to popularize and commercialize. In the twenties, for example, the yellow journalist Hearst offered Freud a blank check if he would come to Chicago to "psychoanalyze" the homosexual thrill killers Loeb and Leopold. Freud turned him down. What he really wanted was unchallenged prestige as a pioneering scientific researcher. And in Austria and Germany, psychoanalysis never caught on as it did in other countries. Just as the psychoanalytic movement was getting established, the war plunged the European continent into chaos and grinding poverty; and soon after, Hitler came to power, outlawed psychoanalysis, and eventually forced Freud to flee for his life.

Even before Hitler, however, during the first third of the twentieth century, the intellectual climate of Austria and Germany explains Freud's relative lack of influence among his scientific compatriots. Freud's major goal was to identify the connections between mind (our capacity for thought and awareness) and brain (that three-pound organ in our skull), thought and physiology, philosophy and medicine. But his culture was sharply split between the mystical and the positivistic. Because Freud's data base consisted only of dreams by himself and a few neurotic patients, scientists could not readily endorse his findings. Freud used no control groups; no "double-blind" experiments; no truly empirical, quantifiable, replicable research. The idealist philosophers Karl Jaspers and Edmund Husserl attacked Freud's claim to be able to know another person's mind; they complained that the highest human achievements were robbed of their dignity by being called the products of sublimated sex drives (Decker, 324). For their part, research scientists believed that physical malfunctions of the body were the cause of mental illness; they could not agree that mental illness might spring from unconscious thoughts and feelings. Freud himself recognized that the materialistic twentieth century was less ready than the philosophical, mystical nineteenth would have been to accept his explanation that dreams originated in repressed feelings and memories (96). Finally, some medical practitioners doubted Freud's seriousness as a therapist because his name was associated with the then disreputable subject of hypnotism. In 1890 he had advocated hypnosis as therapy in a semipopular medical handbook reissued in 1900 and 1905 (Decker, 293–95). After World War I, it was primarily imaginative authors who adopted Freud's ideas in the German-speaking countries. Psychoanalysis as such proliferated mainly in England, France, and the United States (Decker, 290).

Freud called Carl Gustav Jung his "crown prince," and he ardently hoped Jung would succeed him as leader and defender of the psychoanalytic movement. Among lay people Jung became second only to Freud as the most influential psychologist of his day. In his eighties, after half a century of estrangement from Freud, Jung wrote an even-handed account of the early years of the psychoanalytic movement. It eloquently expresses the great admiration young psychologists felt for Freud; the difficulty they experienced in arguing with him; and their urgent need ultimately to break away and freely develop their own views. Freud was neither autocratic nor undemanding. He was like the affectionate father who insists that his children follow in his footsteps because he is sincerely convinced that what is right for him is right for everyone.[6] In his obituary article on Freud, Jung called *The Interpretation of Dreams* "epoch-making . . . probably the boldest attempt ever made to master the enigma of the unconscious psyche on the apparently firm ground of empiricism. . . . For us young psychiatrists it was a fount of illumination."[7] Jung rejected Freud's emphasis on sexuality, and ultimately came to feel that Freud was repressing his own religious yearnings. Nor did Jung agree that dreams were *trying* to conceal anything, although he valued Freud's insight that the dream was the product of repressed feelings emerging in disguise. He felt Freud's greatest achievement was in taking patients seriously, getting to understand their point of view, overcoming numerous prejudices and social hypocrisies, and discovering a privileged access to the unconscious along the royal road of dreams.[8]

A READING

4

Defining Sleep
and Dreams

Before we can interpret dreams, we have to understand what they are. And as soon as we try to answer that question we run into the age-old, vexing, and perhaps insoluble "mind-brain problem." What *is* the relationship between our thoughts and feelings and the brain, that organ behind our forehead? How much of our mental life is a response to what happens inside our brain? Inside the rest of our body? Outside our body? All three of those places send us impressions. How do those impressions interact? How much of our mental functioning is the same as animals'? And to what extent is the human brain unique?

When Freud wrote *The Interpretation of Dreams* between 1897 and 1899 he thought that dreams were infrequent, long-prepared clusters of images that went off like fireworks during sleep, fueled by repressed wishes from early childhood. How valid is his definition of the dream in the light of what we know about sleep and dreams today? If we modify his definition of the dream, must the remainder of his dream theories be modified as well? The rest of our book will address these questions.

Scientists have three ways of studying dreams. They can observe the body to see whether it is active or inactive. They can measure "brain waves" (electrical activity in the brain) with an electroenceph-alogram (EEG) that leaves traces on a moving band of paper. And they can ask for verbal reports from people who have been asleep. The more highly evolved the creature they study, the more sources of information they have.

During sleep an animal is mainly motionless and quiet, in a posture peculiar to its species (lying, standing, perching, hanging). In most species sleep and waking alternate in a twenty-four-hour cycle. This is called a circadian (daylong) rhythm, and it ordinarily is synchronized with another circadian rhythm—the rise and fall of body temperature. In a human the highest daily temperature tends to occur during the middle third of the waking period; the lowest, during the middle third of the sleeping period. The sleep cycle is secondarily influenced by, but not dependent on, external factors like light intensity and environmental temperature, or internal ones like body chemistry, body temperature, hunger, thirst, and muscle fatigue.

Activity burns calories and accumulates toxic waste products in the muscles, producing fatigue. Rest (about four hours a day in humans) is biologically necessary to allow the body to dispose of these toxins and also to limit energy expenditure. Roughly speaking, the higher the metabolic rate—the harder the body's energy-producing systems run—the more rest an animal needs. Small animals have faster heart and breathing rates than big ones. So bats sleep almost twenty hours a day; most grazing animals, from two to four. Normal sleep duration for adult humans ranges from six and a half to nine and a half hours a day, although on the average pregnant women require two hours' more sleep than other people.

Some animals have strange sleep patterns indeed. The blind dolphins of the Indus River sleep seven hours a day, but only in ninety-second snatches, so as to avoid injury from being dashed against the rocks by the strong currents. The bottlenose dolphin and the Black Sea porpoise remain fully awake for one hour and then sleep for two more hours with one hemisphere of their brain at a time. Like humans, these three species of mammals have highly developed cerebral cortices (the location of the most complex brain processes). Some researchers have speculated that these bizarre strategies for getting sleep show that sleep is essential for resting and restoring the cortex—but as yet we lack the technology to prove this theory by observing in sufficient detail the chemistry of the living brain.[1]

Sleep and rest are different. During sleep the electrical activity in the brain changes, and a stronger stimulus of at least some of the senses is needed to make an animal respond.[2] Sleep deprivation has effectively been used in "brainwashing" to make prisoners temporarily psychotic, but no one has proven that sleep, as opposed to rest, is essential for survival, and if so, why. Many chemical substances can make people and animals fall asleep, but no experimenter has conclusively demonstrated that sleep is naturally caused by the accumulation of certain substances in the body, or that the body uses sleep (as opposed to rest) to dispose of certain substances.[3]

Sleep looks like a simple process to the casual observer. But brain-wave measurements have shown that the more advanced the animal, the more varied is the observable electrical activity of its sleeping brain. The brains of invertebrates, fish, and amphibians are too primitive to allow us to tell whether they sleep at all. They may just alternate between active and quiet wakefulness. Even with reptiles, we cannot be sure.[4] Birds and mammals, which probably each evolved separately from reptiles, alternate between "active" or "paradoxical" sleep and "quiet sleep." During quiet sleep the EEG record displays slow, high voltage waves. During active sleep it displays low voltage, uneven electrical impulses accompanied by irregular heart rate, faster breathing, occasional twitching of the legs, loss of muscle tone in the neck and chin, rapid eye movements behind the closed lids, and the loss of the body's ability to regulate its temperature by generating extra heat at need.

Birds' active sleep episodes last only three to fifteen seconds and take up at most 10 percent of sleep time. In mammals they take up from 7 to 46 percent. The more highly evolved the mammal, the more quiet sleep patterns it has: rats have one, cats have two, the higher primates and humans have three. A newborn human does not show all the adult brain-wave patterns until she is about ten weeks old; the different stages of sleep cannot be clearly distinguished on the EEG until a child is one year old.[5]

Human sleep falls into a four-stage cycle of brain activity that lasts about ninety-six minutes and then repeats throughout the night. Its quiet phases are usually called NREM (pronounced "nonrem") sleep, and its active phase, REM ("rapid eye movement") sleep. While a person is falling asleep, her irregular waking brain-wave patterns fall into the characteristic, even "alpha-wave" pattern of meditation or relaxed wakefulness, at about ten cycles a second. "Stage 1" sleep comes next, with low amplitude waves of fast mixed frequencies. The eyes start rolling slowly from side to side, providing one of the most reliable signs of the beginnings of sleep. "Stage 2" starts after a few minutes. Its EEG record is characterized by sleep spindles (one- to two-second bursts of rapid medium-energy waves) and "K complexes" (isolated high amplitude waves), both found only in the higher primates and never during wakefulness. A few minutes later "Stage 3" begins and typically lasts about ten minutes. This stage is dominated by repeating high amplitude waves called "delta waves." When these delta waves occur more than half the time, we are said to be in "Stage 4" sleep. Now it is the most difficult to rouse the dreamer; it may take several minutes; children may be impossible to awaken. Stage 4 is when bed-wetting, sleepwalking, talking in one's sleep, and "night terrors" (see below) may occur. During Stage 4 the brain has an increased senstivity to outside stimuli, but these are not translated into conscious awareness in the usual way. After thirty to forty minutes of total sleep time the body shifts position and brain activity moves back through Stage 3 and Stage 2 (old people may skip the "ascending" Stage 3). Then, some seventy to eighty minutes after sleep onset, REM sleep begins with its paralysis of the voluntary muscles and its vivid dreams. Now the brain-wave response to outside stimuli resembles that of the waking brain.[6] REM lasts about ten minutes and then the whole cycle begins again. It occurs about four times during the night. As the night wears on, Stage 4 periods become shorter while REM episodes become longer. In the early morning REM sleep may last up to an hour, and the accompanying activity of the autonomic nervous system (fast breathing and heartbeat) becomes most intense. After the last REM period of the night no more Stage 4 sleep appears—often, only Stage 2.[7] About 22 percent of human sleep time on the average is spent in the REM condition, compared to 50 percent in Stage 2, 14 percent in Stage 4, and 7 percent each in Stages 1 and 3. Premature infants spend three quarters of the time in REM sleep; full-term newborns, half; this decreases until it approaches adult levels around age five.[8] As we age the total amount of Stage 4 sleep decreases and we briefly waken more often.

REM sleep is characterized by "saw-tooth waves" of medium amplitude, more regular than those of any other phase. The electrooculogram (EOG) now records eye movements at times more rapid and precise than those we can perform voluntarily while awake. REM sleep often coincides with erections of the clitoris or penis because both REM and erections reflect bodily arousal. Both sexes average three or four erections for a total of about two hours a night, regardless of whether they have had sex recently while awake. This happens even to newborns (and to monkeys). Nine-tenths of the erections are accompanied by REM, and seven-tenths of the time the REM period begins before the erection. But REM sleep does not cause erections; and unless one has an orgasm, dream content remains independent of sexual excitation during sleep. If you awaken a person with an erection, she or he will not report more dreams about sex than at other times. (Freud would say that the sexual content had been disguised.) On the other hand, anxious or hostile dreams will inhibit erections during sleep.[9]

The beginning of a sustained scientific effort to link dreaming physiologically to sleep came in 1952. A graduate student named Eugene Aserinsky, working in Nathaniel Kleitman's famous sleep research lab at the University of Chicago, noticed that sleepers' eyes went into episodes of rapid, jerky motion several times during the night. When awakened at such times, the sleepers usually reported that they had been having a vivid dream. At other times, early studies suggested, they did not dream.

The first night in the unfamiliar laboratory setting did distort dreaming. Subjects had less REM sleep and they dreamed about laboratories more. These effects faded after the first night. But the lab experience continued to inhibit nightmares, bizarre dreams, and wet dreams.[10] After a while, however, home recording devices became capable of detecting the onset of REM sleep and then after a certain interval awakening the dreamer. The hope was that every dream during the night could be detected and collected. Researchers wanted to learn whether REM sleep caused dreams, or dreams caused REM sleep, or whether a third factor caused them both.

As the research reports mounted up, it gradually became clear that the vivid, emotionally charged dreams recalled by Freud and his patients were more the exception than the rule. Most dreams were rather banal. Furthermore, intense "REM-type" dreams sometimes happened during other stages of sleep, and fragmentary sequences of dream imagery were common, especially during sleep onset. During awakenings from Stages 1–4 sleep, subjects often reported musing about something or seeing an isolated image. The ideation of the sleeping mind is not entirely extinguished outside REM periods: something seems to be going on in our heads almost all the time.[11]

The most recent research strongly suggests that in addition to musing and single images during sleep there are at least four distinct kinds of dreams, each with its own biochemical hallmark. There are ordinary dreams, and then three other kinds, all of which entail intense anxiety: nightmares, night terrors, and the recurring dreams of post-traumatic stress syndrome.[12] The three types of anxiety dreams gave Freud endless trouble as he tried to fit them into his theory that dreams are wish fulfillments (see chapter 7).

Dreams in general appear to be associated with changes in the brain's balance of four biochemical receptors of stimuli: acetylcholine levels increase; norepinephrine and serotonin levels decrease. Nightmares may increase dopamine levels as well. Patients with angina, high blood pressure, and Parkinson's disease, who are treated with dopamine compounds, may progressively experience more vivid and detailed dreams, then nightmares, and finally, frankly psychotic episodes. Psychotic conditions—schizophrenia in particular—seem to be associated with increased brain dopamine levels, and antipsychotic drugs are nearly all blockers of brain dopamine.

Defining Sleep and Dreams

So vivid nightmares might be said to be on a biochemical continuum halfway between ordinary dreams and psychotic delusions. They usually occur during the second half of the night and during REM sleep. They are clearly remembered as long, frightening, detailed dreams. They may last five to thirty minutes. At the same time, the autonomic nervous system is not excited nearly so much as during night terrors. Adult nightmare sufferers appear to be persons with weak ego boundaries. They are trusting, sensitive, and vulnerable. Often they have unsettled and stormy personal relationships; fluid sexual identities; and jobs as creators, performers, or teachers. Their medical history typically reveals an unusual sensitivity to drugs, allergies, and a tendency to schizophrenic or schizotypal (withdrawn, superstitious, eccentric) personality traits. They often have a family history of schizophrenia. But they seem free of neurotic symptoms such as phobias, anxiety, dissociative and conversion states, or obsessive-compulsive disorders.

Night terrors, on the other hand, usually happen within two hours of when sleep begins. They arise from Stage 3 or 4 rather than from REM sleep. They involve a simple awakening in terror, often accompanied by screaming, sweating, and a dramatic increase in pulse and breathing rates during the fifteen to sixty seconds of awakening. Once awake the victim remembers nothing except sometimes a single vague, frightening image of something weighing down on, closing in on, or choking her or him. The condition seems to be a "disorder of arousal" and it does not respond to the drugs used to treat nightmares. Adult sufferers from night terrors may suffer from phobias or obsessions and tend to suppress strong feelings. Brain injury, brain disease, or temporal lobe epilepsy may produce night terrors. So may abuse of drugs or alcohol, whereas depressants like alcohol and barbiturates inhibit nightmares.

Post-traumatic stress syndrome nightmares differ from both the other types. They can come during any stage of sleep. Like nightmares, they are vividly remembered, but unlike nightmares they repeat without change night after night (example: a sniper fires at you and you see the bullet coming closer and closer until it is just about to strike your head). Restructuring the repeated dream through hypnotic suggestions sometimes helps, but no single form of treatment invariably cures this condition, which may persist indefinitely. The younger and more inexperienced person under twenty, still forming a mature identity, is at much greater risk for incurring such nightmares than is an older victim of combat, rape, and other forms of violence and abuse. In sum, each of the three types of anxiety dreams—although all are aggravated by fatigue and stress—appears to arise from a unique combination of hereditary predisposition, brain chemistry, and life experience.

After this survey we can see that Freud's theories may not apply to the isolated images and to the banal pondering of workaday events that have been found to occupy much of our sleep. Such impressions are immediately forgotten, and Freud dealt only with dreams vivid enough to be remembered upon waking. Nor do his theories seem to apply to the special, dramatic, spectacular disorders of the three types of anxiety dreams. Freud's definition of the dream does exclude one of these, the nonvisual night terrors.[13] By *dream* he means a series of mental images experienced during sleep. Whether or not these are bizarre or distorted, they are hallucinatory: they are unreal phenomena experienced as if they were real. As for nightmares and the recurring dreams of post-traumatic stress syndrome, Freud did not draw upon them for examples in *The Interpretation of Dreams*. He tried to deal with them there and elsewhere only in theory: he stretched his theory too far in an attempt to cover everything, but that does not invalidate it for nonanxiety dreams.

5

The Origins of Psychoanalysis

Freud's first love was biology. And his first publications were in neurology, the study of the nervous system. After six years, he reluctantly abandoned research to become a doctor because his teacher Ernst Brücke had warned him that he could not expect a full-time university teaching position. He became a "brain doctor." But many of the patients who went to see such a specialist were suffering from mental rather than physical illness. To be effective with them, Freud learned that he had to discuss feelings rather than administer physiological tests and prescribe medicines. Because of his background, Freud still hoped to be able to explain these feelings in terms of physiology, to show how they were related to the operations of the body. Brücke left a lasting impression on Freud, and Brücke's ideas on physiology were inspired by the physics of Helmholtz. The ideal was to observe, quantify, predict, and control all phenomena, including our thoughts and feelings. Freud believed that "everything that occurs to the mind is determined."[1]

In this tradition, Freud's sketch of a "Project for a Scientific Psychology" sent to his friend Fliess in 1895—shortly before he began writing *The Interpretation of Dreams*—attempted to describe the mind as a system of nerve cells (neurons or neurones) that governed all mental activity by storing and discharging energy. The total quantity of energy in the system remained constant, but it was concentrated first in one location and then in another within the brain.[2] In *The Interpretation of Dreams* these views are reflected by the frequent use of the terms *cathexis* (the attachment of energy to a particular object) and *innervation* (the discharge of energy). They also appear in Freud's underlying assumption—most obvious in chapter 7—that the psyche can best be understood with the aid of an "economic" model that conceives of psychic energy as distributed and shifting among the "systems" of the mind (consciousness, preconsciousness, and the unconscious), from which it may finally be discharged in the form of muscular activity or ideas.

Freud thought the ultimate source of this energy was sexual. He believed that the body produced a chemical—today we would probably identify it as the sex hormones—that caused sexual tension while simultaneously fueling the nervous system. To ensure our mental and physical health this chemical had to be maintained at moderate levels, Freud affirmed. Masturbation would deplete the body's supply of it and cause neurasthenia ("nervous exhaustion"). Sexual deprivation would allow it to build up in excess, poisoning the body and producing anxiety neurosis. Early sexual traumas could cause psychic conflicts that would misdirect sexual energy and discharge it inappropriately in the form of "conversion symptoms" (wishes expressed as physical symptoms) or obsessional delusions or phobias. In other words, a faulty discharge of sexual tension would be exclusively physical or exclusively mental rather than a balance of the two. Freud applied this theory to women as well as to men, but it was implicitly the product of a male imagination focused on the accumulation of sperm and its discharge during male orgasm. Freud probably did not imagine how female orgasm might discharge toxic chemicals. But he was sure that blocked or misdirected sexuality was the foundation of mental illness.[3] That is why he speculated that unconscious sexual wishes provided the motivating force for dreams: he saw dreams as closely related to neurotic symptoms, although dreams occurred in healthy as well as mentally ill people.

The Origins of Psychoanalysis

So Freud believed that consciousness was the subjective aspect of concrete physical processes in the nervous system. He did not claim that our thoughts and feelings were caused by physical processes, but he believed that they were bound to them and could not occur separately (Jones 1:368–69).[4] In other words, Freud did not believe in an immortal soul that could exist independently of the body. Over his long career, Freud evolved slowly into a philosopher. He never abandoned the conviction that the mind's activities are ultimately related to and interdependent with those of the body. But he gave up his initial search to establish precisely what those connections were as he came to admit that the mind/body problem was insoluble in the present state of scientific knowledge. In time, he even made fun of those who hoped for an easy solution. As he wryly exclaimed to Jung in 1908: "I believe that if [some professors of psychiatry] were analyzed it would turn out that they are still waiting for the discovery of the bacillus or protozoon of hysteria as for the messiah who must after all come some day to all true believers. . . . Then we shall be able to leave psychol' ⸱y to the writers."[5] But Freud still hoped that his research might contribute to an eventual solution. With *The Interpretation of Dreams* he was like an engineer who had started tunneling through the mountainous problem of human mental activity from the brain (organic) side, but then moved around to tunnel from the opposite, mind (mental) side.

In order to try to understand illnesses that seemed to have neither a physical cause nor a physical cure, Freud made himself into the first psychoanalyst in history. At the time he was writing *The Interpretation of Dreams,* he believed that mental illness arose from a three-stage process: (1) frustration or inhibition of desire; (2) fixation of thwarted desire on an infantile object; (3) repression of the infantile desire by the developing conscious self (ego), which cannot accept it.[6] But such repressed desire never can be destroyed; it continually struggles to break free of its restraints; the efforts of repression must be everlastingly renewed. When its energies are occupied by such repression, the ego becomes unavailable for deep, lasting, mature attachments. Neurosis, then, would be the outward sign not only of sexual deprivation but also of a hidden aversion to sexuality and an inability to love. The repressed impulses themselves are not a simple adult desire for sexual intercourse, but rather, primitive forms of erotic responsiveness inherited from infancy. Freud saw neurotic symptoms as compromises between impulses and inhibitions. He found that people clung to their symptoms because they offered the primary gain of achieving libidinal gratification of repressed desires through the hallucinatory device of the symptom—replacing sexual perversions and incestuous encounters with less frightening substitutes—and the secondary gains from exploiting the illness itself in order to avoid painful situations and to receive additional attention. The symptoms allowed the possibility of acting out repressed desires in disguised form. For instance, hysterical convulsions could imitate the movements of the body during sexual intercourse.

Freud's psychotherapy sought to lead the patient toward a greater self-awareness that could alleviate neurotic symptoms. Infantile desires had to be brought to the surface of consciousness. Once the patient realized that these desires were neither horrible or possible, they might be neutralized. Then the patient's libido (instinctive desire) could be more constructively redirected. "Every psychoanalytic treatment," he said, "is an attempt at liberating repressed love which has found a meagre outlet in the compromise of a symptom."[7]

The relationship between Freud and his analysands was not as one-sided as the relationship between a physically ill person and a doctor. Freud saw his patients as his partners in exploring the unconscious: each needed the other. His starting point was patients' dreams because he believed and repeatedly stated that "the interpretation of dreams is the royal road to a knowledge of the unconscious activities of the mind" (647). Freud's first recorded dream analysis occurred on 4 March 1895—a lazy medical student tried to avoid having to get up by dreaming that he was already at work in the hospital. The first complete analysis of a dream that he admitted to be his own was written on 24 July 1895. This is the famous "Dream of Irma's Injection," otherwise known as "the specimen [a more modest and accurate translation is 'sample'] dream of psychoanalysis" (see 138–54). Freud first spoke of writing a book about dreams in May 1897, and it was composed from 1898 through September 1899. The 1901 "Fragment of an Analysis of a Case of Hysteria" (published 1905) forms a sequel to *The Interpretation of Dreams.* It focuses on how two dreams reveal the sources of the patient "Dora's" suffering, and for the first time inserts dream interpretation into the context of a psychoanalysis (Jones 1:353–63). After twenty more years of clinical practice Freud had no doubt that in psychoanalysis dream interpretation brought far more of the repressed to light than did any other method.[8]

Freud further came to believe that the best way of becoming a psychoanalyst was by studying one's own dreams.[9] He began his study of dreams with the person he knew best: himself. When he had completed *The Interpretation of Dreams* he realized that he had been recording the first psychoanalysis in history. Like Dante's hero in the *Divine Comedy* Freud undertook a lonely, terrifying pilgrimage toward knowledge, willingly confronting purgatorial and hellish visions so that he could master them in preparation for freeing others also.[10]

Although the relationship between dreams and mental illness is one of Freud's main presuppositions, he deals with this topic only briefly in *The Interpretation of Dreams.* He treats the vivid remembered dreams of ordinary people as expressions of universal human conflicts. He had already analyzed more than a thousand dreams during analytic sessions with his patients. But he avoids reporting overtly neurotic or psychotic dreams because to explain them, he feels he would need to provide a lengthy case history for each patient; besides, he does not want to lay himself open to the charge that his examples are aberrant and that no valid conclusions regarding the dreams of normal people can be drawn from them. He mixes his own dreams in with those of acquaintances or anonymous patients, sometimes disguising the former as the latter.

Freud was so reserved and almost secretive about his private life that he did not want even his closest friends to know the date of his wedding anniversary (Jones 2:408–9). In his book he suppresses most allusions to his own family, not to mention any discussion of his sexual feelings or the infantile fantasies that his theory says provide the primary motivating force for dreams. He does not trust his readers, and he admits it (138 n. 2). A letter to Wilhelm Fliess speaks of the shock he experienced on surprising his mother naked in a train when he was a little boy;[11] but since she lived until 1930 he did not wish publicly to reveal whatever sexual feelings he may have had toward her. And he seems to have been so inhibited by repressed rivalry toward his father that he could not even begin his self-analysis, much less *The Interpretation of Dreams*, until after his father had died. Needless to say, we readers have no call to feel superior. We all have similar problems; Freud faced them and surmounted them as much as a frail human can. Courage is not heedlessness, but fear that has been overcome.

However reticent Freud may have been regarding his emotional life, he was open and unaffected about his intellectual life. He revised *The Interpretation of Dreams* for thirty-five years, frankly admitting his difficulties, doubts, and dissatisfaction with his ideas. In fact, he enlivens his book by dramatizing his struggle for understanding: he creates an imaginary debate with his readers. He has them raise objections that he then answers. And from one edition to the next, he allows his earlier ideas and enthusiasms to stand in order to reveal the evolution of his thought. He uses footnotes to update and to correct himself, or inserts new paragraphs to show how what he has just said now seems inadequate. So Jung's influence makes itself felt in the second edition, of 1909; Stekel's views on universal symbolism become prominent in the third edition, of 1911; Ferenczi and Rank become the dominant figures from the fourth edition, of 1914, on. Freud's *Three Essays on the Theory of Sexuality* (1905) was the only other work to which he paid nearly this much sustained attention.

Freud's views of mental structure and dynamics become fully explicit only years later (notably in *The Ego and the Id*), but they are essential for understanding *The Interpretation of Dreams*. His key idea is the unconscious. He knew that most people considered "conscious" and "mental" to be the same thing; he wanted to extend the concept of "mental" to include areas that are not conscious.[12] He stressed that mental activity can occur without our realizing it. In the wake of writers like Rousseau, Chateaubriand, Nerval, Novalis, and Nietzsche, he realized that our earliest impressions, although consciously forgotten, remain dynamically active throughout life; they influence how we experience the present. Freud certainly did not "discover" the unconscious, but he made it into a scientific concept susceptible of methodical investigation. And he introduced a crucial distinction between "preconscious" and "unconscious." The first is forgotten but accessible; the second is repressed and inaccessible except under the prolonged guidance of psychoanalysis, and it can enter our awareness only in disguise.

To make the structure of the mind more intelligible, Freud introduced a number of comparisons with everyday life. The first would later come to be known as the "layer-cake model" of the psyche. According to this metaphor, layers of impressions accumulate one on top of the other throughout our life. Like strata of geological sediment, our infantile memories and impulses become progressively overlaid with more recent experiences. They become deeply buried but not destroyed. Dreams can reactivate them because a prime characteristic of dreams is "hypermnesia," an especially keen capacity for recall. Dreams unearth infantile selfishness, terror, and rage that in waking adult life we have long since left behind. "Dreaming is on the whole an example of regression to the dreamer's earliest condition, a revival of his childhood, of the instinctual impulses which dominated it and of the methods of expression which were then available to him" (587).

The limitation of the layer-cake model is that it does not convey the idea of a continual struggle between expression and repression that Freud finds characteristic of the psyche. To suggest this conflict, Freud commonly uses battlefield metaphors in his writing. His concept of the opposing forces is not fully developed at the time of the earlier editions of *The Interpretation of Dreams,* but eventually he characterizes them as an unconscious, infantile "id" opposed by an unconscious "superego." The id is fueled by libido, "the name of the force . . . by which the [sexual] instinct manifests itself." Freud specified elsewhere that "sexual" does not necessarily mean "genital": it can also refer to more primitive forms of erotic gratification—oral or anal—encountered early in child development.[13] The superego develops from commands and moral teaching directed at the child by parents and significant others in his or her life; gradually these are internalized. They become second nature, while awareness of their original source is lost. The superego can appear in one of two roles, or both at once. It can be a beneficent conscience guiding a person toward mature civilized behavior that shows respect for others. Or it can be an unyielding, punishing standard (Karen Horney's "tyranny of the shoulds") against which a person measures him- or herself only to fall short like a child criticized by harsh, demanding parents. The ego, like a colorless referee, attempts to arbitrate and reach a compromise among the opposing demands of id, superego, and external reality. The ego contains our conscious self-concept; it tries to be practical and realistic.[14] Working together, the ego and the positive superego try to channel the energy of the libido, "sublimating" it by redirecting it toward "higher" goals such as work, creativity, or altruistic service. In another famous metaphor, Freud compared the id to the capitalist who provides the funds for a business venture, and the ego or superego (although sometimes, too, the id itself) as the entrepreneur who invests those funds and puts them to work (599–600).

Freud hit on his definitive metaphor only ten years later. Neither the layer-cake nor the battlefield illustrates how an unwelcome impulse can be expelled from conscious awareness; continue to struggle to reenter; and meanwhile indirectly make its presence felt through symptoms, disguised fantasies, and other disturbances in waking life. In Freud's "Five Lectures on Psychoanalysis" (1910) he asks us to imagine a disorderly person (the id-impulse) who disrupts a lecture (the routines of daily living) and is expelled by several strong men (the superego) who then bar the door with their chairs (inhibitions) so that the troublemaker cannot return. But you can still hear muffled shouts and poundings from the hall (the unconscious). So the lecture still is disrupted; the task of psychoanalysis is to serve as mediator and peacemaker, talking to the troublemaker and allowing it to reenter the lecture hall (awareness) on condition that it behave acceptably (be acknowledged as a feeling without insisting on being "acted out" in the form of antisocial, destructive or self-destructive behavior).[15]

Sleep complicates this situation. During sleep the censorship of the ego and superego relaxes. The repressed unconscious becomes more independent of the restraining forces. It slips out of their grasp and, not wishing to remain inactive, exploits the reduction of censorship by constructing a forbidden but disguised dream drama out of the impressions of the previous day.[16]

To put it yet another way, the preconscious is like a beach lying between consciousness and the unconscious. While we are awake it is flooded by the high tide of impressions from the outside world, and consequently ignored. But it becomes exposed during the ebb tide of sleep. All the fleeting impressions and insignificant details to which we paid no attention during the day now become available as raw materials for the untiring, ingenious id. But censorship remains sufficiently strong so that the id's impulses can emerge only in heavily veiled forms.

The homey quality of all these comparisons may suggest some of the flavor of Freud's clear, down-to-earth writing. Yet any translation severely distorts his thought. He was a master of German nuances, colloquialisms, puns, and allusions to late nineteenth-century Vienna that cannot really be reproduced in another language. Worse yet, the English translation by Strachey emphasizes the technical, medical, and mechanistic dimensions of Freud's theory at the expense of the everyday, philosophical, and mystical.[17] Strachey borrowed unfamiliar words from Latin—*Ego* and *Id*—to render *das Ich* and *das Es*. Actually, the best translations here would be "the I" and "the It." Since *das Kind* (child) is a neuter noun in German, children growing up in that language often hear themselves referred to as "it" during a stage of their development that corresponds to the uncivilized, unsocialized, archaic impulsive regions of the adult psyche. The highfalutin word *cathexis* (unconscious emotional charge) loses all the familiarity of its German counterpart, *Besetzung*. *Besitzt* (cathected) is the commonest way of saying that a seat or place is "taken" or occupied; the word appears on the outside of a public restroom door when you push the bolt closed.

In the Vienna of 1900, Freud invented the word *Psychoanalyse* to describe his new enterprise because he wanted clearly to suggest to his readers that he was doing an analysis of the psyche or soul—meaning for Freud the essential self, the core of the personality. Where Freud's German refers to the structure and organization of the soul (using the adjective *seelische,* meaning "pertaining to the soul"), the English substitutes the bland word *mental.* Contrary to Freud's often-declared intention, the Anglo-Saxon establishment wanted psychoanalysis to become an exclusively medical specialty. "Soul" lacked the aura of scientific respectability that many practitioners of the struggling new discipline craved. Finally, the very title of Freud's masterwork, *Die Traumdeutung,* is deliberately provocative because it had been used for popular "dreambooks" that claimed to disclose the future. Thus Freud reveals from the outset that he intends to show us something hidden behind a facade. More important, he challenges us: he knows that we may not think dreams worthy of serious scientific consideration, but he will prove otherwise.[18]

6

Manifest Content:
The Facade of
Dreams

Dreams and delusions, Freud holds, spring from what has been repressed. A dream disguises an infantile wish—which may attract more
recent, adult wishes to it—so that it can evade our censorious conscience and be fulfilled harmlessly in fantasy. Thus dreams provide a
safe outlet for the impulses of our premoral self (588–92).[1] It bears
repeating that with few exceptions in *The Interpretation of Dreams*,
Freud does not trace his examples back to the underlying infantile
wish. He could have done so, but he wishes to avoid indiscretions
concerning himself, and to avoid lengthy reports of the analytic process leading to the disclosure of such wishes in his patients. His two
longest chapters, occupying more than half the book, deal with the
secondary materials swept up by the powerful, concealed wishful impulse, and with the ways in which these materials are then blended
and molded together to mask that impulse. What we first encounter
when we attempt to understand dreams is the latent wish's mask; a
facade; the "manifest content" that is the dream as told by the
dreamer; a verbal translation of visual images that are themselves a
disguise. The "dream-work," the process of concealment, uses any materials at hand to build the dream's facade. It has four major sources

of supply. Two of these are obvious: bodily sensations during sleep and the "day residue" (recent memories; especially, impressions from the previous day). The other two are less obvious: childhood memories and universal human experiences.

BODILY SENSATIONS

"The Pepperoni Pizza Theory" is one of the most popular explanations of dreams—the notion that vivid dreams come from indigestion caused by eating lots of rich, spicy food. Freud allows that the stimulation or irritation of a body organ may contribute to a dream, but adds that you cannot predict what the content of that dream will be. (You will recall that nearly all REM sleep is accompanied by an erection of the clitoris or penis, but that actual orgasm must occur in sleep before you are certain to have a sexual dream.) For example, at a time when Freud had a large boil at the base of his scrotum, was feverish and exhausted, and found it painful even to walk, you would have expected him to have disagreeable dreams elicited by his discomfort. Instead, he had a pleasant dream of riding gracefully on horseback. In waking life, no activity would have been more impossible for him. When his perineum began to get irritated during the night under the soothing dressing that had allowed Freud to get to sleep, the dream-work functioned as the "guardian of sleep" by transforming the feeling of pressure from the dressing into the sensation of sitting on a saddle so that the feeling would not wake him up. Furthermore, the dream fulfilled the wish to be well by allowing Freud to imagine himself doing something he could have done only when fully recovered: thus the dream vigorously denied his illness. Another time, when Freud was vacationing in the Tyrol, the dream-work forestalled his waking up by transforming the loud pealing of church bells outside into a hallucination that the pope was dead. Freud says these are "dreams of convenience": when a physical impression becomes too strong to be entirely ignored by the sleeper, then the dream will attempt either to deny it or to transform it into something else consistent with sleeping. Painful sensations during sleep may be combined with pleasant ones so as to blunt them—as in the morning dreams that combine the pressure of a full bladder with sexual arousal. Freud claims that every dream in part fulfills the ego's wish to go on sleeping (263–68).

THE "DAY RESIDUE"

Freud explains that dreams prefer impressions from the past few days, and that they select minor impressions that have passed unnoticed during waking life, rather than—like our waking memory—retaining what is most important (197). From the day residue, the dream seems to choose elements that have not been "processed" by consciousness during the day: overlooked, interrupted, unresolved, or repressed thoughts, and preconscious thoughts that have stirred up elements from the unconscious (593). As Freud understands it, sleep is a narcissistic (self-loving) withdrawal to a state of total self-absorption. In sleep the ego wishes to sink back into itself. But unprocessed materials from the day residue have remained semi-independent of the ego. They subsist as potential irritants, as distractions from narcissism. So they are exploited by the lurking unconscious, instinctual impulses that are always waiting to find an outlet and to sneak into our awareness.[2]

Freud analyzes his own "Dream of the Botanical Monograph" to illustrate how dreams transform the day residue. "I had written a monograph on a certain plant. The book lay before me and I was at the moment turning over a folded colored plate. Bound up in each copy there was a dried specimen of the plant, as though it had been taken from a herbarium" (202). He traces the dream back to two recent memories. The day before, he had seen a new study of *The Genus Cyclamen* in the window of a bookstore. He remembered that cyclamen was his wife's favorite flower, and he reproached himself for not bringing some home to her more often. In turn this reminds him of a friend of his wife's, a former patient who had seen her and asked after

Freud two days earlier. Once long before, this patient's husband had found her crying because he had forgotten the flowers he always used to bring her on her birthday. He offered to go buy a bouquet right away, but she could not be consoled because she realized she was no longer so important to him as she once had been.

A second train of thought leads to a more significant day residue concealed by the first: a recent intense conversation between Freud and the eye surgeon Dr. Königstein. They were discussing a patient named Flora ("flower") when they were interrupted by a Dr. Gärtner ("gardener") and his wife; Freud congratulated them on their "blooming" look. In the unconscious these three elements—flower, gardener, blooming—served to link the memory of the conversation with the memory of seeing the book on flowers. Typically, the connection of the two memories is "overdetermined": several impressions work together to reinforce it although fewer might have sufficed. Such a wealth of connections is typical in the elaboration of dreams and fantasies.

The association between flower (the book in the store window) and medicine (the conversation with Dr. Königstein) receives further reinforcement when Freud remembers that his own first important monograph was devoted to the medical properties of cocaine (which comes from a plant). He realized that the drug had anesthetic properties and mentioned this in his publication. But then he went off to see his fiancée for three weeks before doing the clinching experiments that would have been needed to establish Freud's claim to having discovered a new anesthetic. Since another researcher quickly performed such experiments and reported on them, Freud had in effect sacrificed fame for love.[3]

But now fame beckoned to Freud again. He had sent part of the manuscript of *The Interpretation of Dreams* to his friend Fliess for evaluation. Fliess had written back a glowing evaluation and said that he could imagine holding the finished book in his hands and turning its pages (March 1898, two days before Freud's dream). Freud does not spell out the implications here, but it appears that the dream chose the recent image of the botanical monograph to gratify Freud's wish for fame: once before he had missed his chance to achieve greatness with a book on a flower (the coca plant), but this time he will succeed in capturing a flower (his current psychoanalytic patient, Flora) between the pages of a book on dreams.

Still another chain of associations points to an unacceptable infantile wish that Freud does not disclose. He forgets to bring his wife her favorite flower, but she is more considerate in remembering to bring him his "favorite flowers"—artichokes. To eat an artichoke, you pull off the leaves one by one. This gesture reminds Freud of when he and his sister were given an illustrated book by their father and allowed to pull it to pieces like an artichoke. Freud was then five; this is almost his only visual memory retained from so early in life. Given his hint elsewhere (224), one may suspect that it is a "screen memory" (an invented, composite one concealing a host of associated but less admissible impressions) reflecting the infantile wish to masturbate— an activity that Freud elsewhere called "the first addiction."⁴

Anticipating the reader's objections to his interpretation of the "Dream of the Botanical Monograph," Freud asks: what if Dr. Gärtner and his "blooming" wife had not interrupted the conversation about Flora? How would the emotional conversation with Dr. Königstein have been represented in the dream if there were no longer enough links to connect it with the disguise of the trivial memory of the botanical monograph? "The dream would simply have been different," Freud answers. "Another indifferent impression of the same day—for crowds of such impressions enter our minds and are then forgotten—would have taken the place of the 'monograph' in the dream, would have linked up with the subject of the conversation and would have represented it in the content of the dream. Since it was in fact the monograph and not any other idea that was chosen to serve this function, we must suppose that it was the best adapted for the connection" (209).

INFANTILE MATERIAL

Freud believes that dreams display hypermnesia—exceptionally keen and full recall. They can draw upon many impressions from childhood that are no longer readily available to waking consciousness: both unrepressed memories stored in the preconscious, and repressed ones stored in the unconscious and emerging only in disguise. Among many examples, Freud reports one of a physician in his thirties who often dreamed of a yellow lion that he could afterwards describe in great detail. At last one day while visiting his childhood home he discovered such a lion in the form of a china ornament that had been lost for many years. His mother told him it had been his favorite childhood toy, although he himself had since forgotten it (223).

But in his discussion of "Infantile Material as a Source of Dreams" (221–53) Freud actually mentions few memories from before the age of five or so. Many he cites date from the dreamers' teens. Later analysts have rushed to fill the gap by speculating on how our earliest childhood shapes our lives. As a general rule, the less hard evidence they have, the more all-encompassing their theories become. Otto Rank traced mental illness back to the "birth trauma," the shock of emerging from the womb. And in the clever *Book of the It*, Georg Groddeck went so far as to claim that we preserve memories of the struggles of the "spermal pack" to reach and penetrate the ovum! More nearly in the mainstream of psychoanalysis are suggestions that the very backdrop of our dreams may derive from "the dream screen," the nursing infant's memories of the blurred breast, which is the last thing it sees as it falls blissfully asleep.[5]

For Freud himself the most important early memories were of "the primal scene"—the child's seeing or overhearing sexual intercourse between his parents or other members of the household. He believed such scenes, disguised, would return frequently in dreams. Originally, children could understand sex only as something violent and uncanny, so they would respond with anxiety (624). In Freud's famous case of the "Wolf Man," a primal scene memory provides the key to the analysis, based on the interpretation of a vivid dream where the patient, then four, saw white wolves sitting in the branches of a walnut tree outside his window.[6]

Psychoanalysis often unearths patients' "screen memories," which may be interpreted as if they were dreams. These are synthetic rather than historically accurate recollections from early childhood. They often seem insignificant, but they conceal powerful feelings and condense many situations in which those feelings were stimulated. Freud identifies two types: a single neutral detail that was once part of a painful scene (a man remembers seeing a basin of ice on a table when he was three; analysis reveals this to be a fragment of the scene of the death of his grandmother), or a harmless early memory that has replaced a later, less innocent one often arising from the sexual tempests of adolescence. An example of the latter told by Freud, and apparently autobiographical, involves a boy of two and a half playing with a girl cousin of his age and a boy cousin a year older in a field full of yellow flowers. All three children gather bouquets, but the girl has the nicest. With an unspoken common accord, the boys fall on her and snatch away her flowers. She runs to the peasant woman who has been looking after them. The woman gives the children bread to comfort the little girl and to settle down the little boys.

This memory had become unconsciously associated with Freud's unspoken love for a girl in a yellow dress (the same color as the flowers) when he was seventeen. Later on, when he and the girl cousin who had been his childhood playmate turned twenty, their families wanted them to marry. The uncle was wealthy; the union would have brought Freud economic security. But the cousins did not fall in love, and for a time Freud's fancy remained fixed on the girl in yellow.[7] From the perspective of mature sexuality, the screen memory symbolically gratifies both the family's wishes and a forbidden fantasy at the same time. Sharing bread with his cousin connotes the economic security that the two families wanted to assure them. But taking the yellow flowers from the girl cousin also represents (with homosexual undertones, because the act is shared with another male) "de-flowering" the desirable girl in yellow.[8]

Not only do dreams' contents draw heavily on infantile memories, Freud believes, but even physiologically dreams are regressive. During waking, the physical impressions we receive move "inward" to be stored up in our memory; during sleep, these stored-up impressions move back "outward" from the memory, once again to become physical impressions—albeit, this time, hallucinatory ones (581). The very form of dreams is determined by our psychic regression to an earlier stage of life and to the means of expression then available to us—visual images and actions rather than words; isolated impressions rather than sustained logic (587). In sum, Freud describes the dream as "*a substitute for an infantile scene modified by being transferred on to a recent experience. The infantile scene is unable to bring about its own revival and has to be content with returning as a dream*" (585; emphasis Freud's). The fabrication of the infantile scene is aided and abetted by repressed wishes that can find expression only by making a detour backwards in time through infantile materials, if they do not originate in those materials to begin with; there, these wishes pick up the disguises that allow them to be represented—under the constraints of censorship—in the preconscious realm of dreams.[9]

UNIVERSAL HUMAN EXPERIENCES

Certain typical dreams experienced by many people are hard to interpret through the use of the dreamer's free associations. They seem to have stereotyped meanings. Dreams of flying, falling, and dizziness may derive from memories of being tossed, carried, or swung about as a child, or from romping and playground equipment—although the adult hands that supported the child are no longer present in the dream (305–6).[10]

Anxiety dreams about taking an examination may result from the fear of some responsibility or test—including a sexual encounter—scheduled for the next day. But from both personal and therapeutic experience, Freud believes that people dream only of examinations that in real life they have already passed, sometimes years before. Thus the latent content of the dream—the meaning discovered through analysis—would be fulfilling a wish and reassuring the dreamer by saying in effect "You see? Just as you succeeded in the examination that you must retake in your anxiety dream, so you shall succeed in the dreaded test that lies before you."[11]

Manifest Content: The Facade of Dreams

Typical dreams of being underclothed or naked and embarrassed in front of strangers seem contradictory because the onlookers invariably seem indifferent. In such dreams, says Freud, the crowd of strangers (for they are never familiar) before whom the dreamer appears stand for the "wishful contrary" to secrecy. That is, they represent something desired by its opposite: secrecy by publicity; the one significant other to whom the child particularly wanted to expose him- or herself by strangers. Without the embarrassment, such situations frequently occur in childhood. But children often feel exhilarated when they can undress themselves; they frequently indulge in exhibitionism. It is our adult psychic censorship that in retrospect arouses the distress accompanying such dreams. Distress allows the dreamer to dissociate him- or herself from the childish, exhibitionistic desire that the dream clandestinely serves to gratify (276–79).

Finally, typical dreams of the death of a loved person, when they are unaccompanied by grief, may portray the wished-for removal of a rival. For a child, death merely means absence. Dreams of a loved one's death do not necessarily reflect the wishes of the present but simply those that may have existed at some point in the past. So they are not as bloodthirsty and abhorrent as they at first seem. Here Freud launches into a discussion of a child's predilection for the parent of the opposite sex and rivalry with the parent of the same sex—notions that were to become one of the cornerstones of the later developments of his psychology. He invokes the contrasting myths of Oedipus and Hamlet. The first acts out in full detail the child's murder of his father and his marriage to his mother: the latter illustrates the severe repression of these selfsame impulses. You could say that all neurotics are either Oedipus or Hamlet (281–301). "Like Oedipus," Freud declares, "we live in ignorance of these wishes, repugnant to morality, which have been forced upon us by Nature, and after their revelation we may all of us well seek to close our eyes to the scenes of our childhood" (297).[12] To demystify Freud's concept of the "Oedipus complex" we should realize that it is theoretically universal: some years later, Freud defined it simply as "the emotional relation of a child to its two parents."[13]

7

Why Dream?
Wish Fulfillment
versus Anxiety

As Freud begins *The Interpretation of Dreams* by reviewing his precursors' work in the long first chapter, his primary concern is to find
support for the idea that dreams—despite appearances—are meaningful. He admits that at first glance dreams seem to focus on precisely
those marginal impressions that waking consciousness has not seen fit
to bother with—the most trivial, insignificant details of everyday life.
When you also take into account dreams' absurdity and incoherence,
it is difficult to see how they could tell us anything worthwhile about
ourselves. They seem like a junkheap of the unimportant. In the glare
of our more intense waking impressions, they fade out quickly. Not
only are most dreams forgotten, but it is hard to ascertain whether
what we remember of dreams is not in fact combined with the more
vivid impressions of waking life (52–55, 78–79).

To buttress his claim that dreams tell us something important
about the dreamer, Freud points out the problems raised by the underlying assumptions of the competing theories of his time. He says
disarmingly that there is no reason dreams should have a purpose: but
because we have the habit of seeking a goal in everything, we shall be
more receptive to theories that claim that dreams are trying to accom-

plish something (107). Freud's use of "we" here is an attempt to ally the reader with him and against the rationalistic Enlightenment and post-Enlightenment traditions that dismissed dreams as meaningless.

Freud identifies three main groups of theories (106–19). According to him, the first says that although the body sleeps, the mind does not. In sleep its full normal functioning continues—of course, in a modified way because the conditions of the state of sleep are different from those of waking. But based on the mere fact that the body is sleeping, such theories encounter problems in explaining all the differences between dreams and waking thought. Moreover, such theories offer no reasons that, during sleep, "the complicated mechanism of the mental apparatus should continue to operate even when set in circumstances for which it appears undesigned" (197).

A second group of theories assumes that sleep confuses and partially paralyzes the mind. Dreaming represents a limited, undisciplined, impaired form of psychic functioning. This theory (wrote Freud in 1899) is the most popular with doctors and scientists. By saying that the mind has been temporarily crippled, it neatly avoids all the difficulties of trying to explain the inner contradictions and incoherence of dreams. Since this theory also holds that dreams result from a partial awakening, it can readily explain variations in their degree of continuity, logic, and realism. The more nearly awake the sleeping mind is, the more like waking thought the dream will become. During the early morning hours, as the body recovers from fatigue, more of our brain cells come awake and therefore dreams become less senseless (109). Like the first group of theories, this second group assumes dreams have no function. They are somatic (bodily) events only—invariably useless and often harmful. Since our sleeping body continues to be bombarded by stimuli from within and without, these continue to produce reactions. But these reactions are random, as different parts of our mind are stimulated in turn. They cannot be interpreted as revealing anything about the dreamer because they always originate from outside her and are in no way determined by her feelings and intentions. (In modern guise, this theory has recently reappeared as the "activation-synthesis hypothesis," of which more shall be said in our conclusion.) A variant of this theory states that dreams arise from impressions of the previous day that were too marginal and unimportant to be dealt with then. Because the mind preserves a memory trace of everything it has perceived, it remains burdened with these impressions. They have elicited mental excitations that must be discharged. During sleep, the superfluous memory traces from the previous day are either "excreted" in the form of dreams or else disposed of by being woven into harmless dream images and then incorporated into the psyche.

The third major group of theories, Freud explains, ascribes a special function to the sleeping mind; grants it special abilities unavailable to the waking mind; and believes that dreaming fulfills some useful purpose. Some see dreams as a form of play; freed from the constraints of waking life, the imagination can refresh us during a sort of holiday. The romantic writers of England, France, and Germany (notably Coleridge, Nodier, Nerval, and Novalis) made more ambitious claims. For them dreaming was a superior state of consciousness; it gave us access to understanding and revelation hidden during the day; the dreamer was inspired. This attitude echoes the belief widespread in classical antiquity and in the Bible, that dreams could bring revelation from the gods or foretell the future. In ancient Greek there were even two separate words—*enhypnion* and *oneiros*—for ordinary as opposed to prophetic dreams.

Freud dismisses all three groups of theories. For him, dreaming is neither equal, inferior, nor superior to the thought processes of waking life: it is different. Dreams are hypermnesic: they often recall something beyond the reach of our waking memory—quite commonly, childhood experiences. Freud gives many examples from other authors' reports, and two examples from his own dreams. He adds: "I am in a position several times a week to prove to patients from their dreams that they are really quite familiar with quotations, obscene works and so on, and make use of them in their dreams, although they have forgotten them in their waking life" (48; see 44–52). Forgotten impressions do not return to the sleeping mind because they are waste products that must be excreted or discharged. If so, why would the same memories keep coming back in dreams, and why would dreams still contain memories from the distant past? Forgotten impressions are attracted and grouped together by a powerful hidden force, like iron filings shaping themselves into swirling patterns under the influence of a concealed magnet.

Many people, says Freud, believe that dreams are caused by sensory impressions during sleep; but then why does a single impression produce many different dreams? He gives the example of three dreams reported by the same person on three mornings when his alarm clock went off. One contained church bells; another, sleighbells; and the third, the crash of falling crockery. Stimuli from internal organs do not produce predictable dream content either. Physical stimuli certainly make impressions that can be woven into an ongoing dream, but we cannot predict how these impressions will be translated into dream images because they are subordinate to the ongoing dream as a preexisting process (56–63, 67–73).

Freud concludes that dreams draw their materials both from past memories and from the present situation of the dreamer. But their essential content is forgotten past impressions. They reveal no transcendence: they have no supernatural sources. And they process their materials differently than rational waking thought does. Trains of thought interrupted, undeveloped, or unsolved during the day are intertwined with material that has been repressed from consciousness— or that has been incited to move from the unconscious to the preconscious during the previous day as the result of a subliminal impression associated with the more distant past (593).

DREAMS AS WISH FULFILLMENTS

"Regression" and "repression" are the keys to Freud's concept of the dream. To prepare us to admit that dreams reveal repressed parts of our thoughts, Freud emphasizes that we have all had immoral dreams. They contain impulses repellent to our conscience. Once again this shows that dreams have access to psychic material that is absent from or minimal in the waking states (100, 103). Unlike other involuntary ideas, which simply seem strange to us, immoral ideas come into direct conflict with another part of our psyche—our sense of right and wrong. Somehow dreams let slip through to awareness fantasies that in ordinary waking life we would immediately deny and repudiate.

Before 1900 other authors—notably Nietzsche—had spoken of repression and of the hypocrisy of "bourgeois morality." But Freud's originality was to specify that immoral dream impulses are survivors from a time when we had no moral sense: our early childhood. At the time these impulses may not have been distressing, but they become distressing in retrospect. The most fundamental of these impulses, Freud believed, was what he was later to call the Oedipus complex, the young child's desire to have sexual contact (as the child understands it) with the parent of the opposite sex, while disposing of the rival parent of the same sex.

To avoid offending readers, and to lead them gently to accept his main hypothesis, Freud uses several parallel strategies. His exposition is nonjudgmental, initially vague, and gradual. He emphasizes that we are not responsible for the immorality of our dreams: it is not chosen and willed. At first he avoids spelling out what he means by infantile fantasies. And he unfolds his master hypothesis by degrees as the reader becomes more experienced in psychoanalytic thinking and better prepared to accept Freud's ideas. At the conclusion of chapter 2 he announces that "when the work of interpretation has been completed, we perceive that a dream is the fulfillment of a wish." Here he carefully invokes the "work of interpretation" to explain why his principle is not intuitively obvious. At the end of chapter 4 he complicates his formula by stating that "a dream is a (disguised) fulfilment of a (suppressed or repressed) wish." Chapter 5 further enriches this idea by bringing in the "layer-cake model" of the psyche: "a succession of meanings or wish-fulfilments may be superimposed on one another, the bottom one being the fulfilment of a wish dating from earliest childhood." But in chapter 7 he tacitly assumes that this infantile wish is the essential one, by no longer mentioning the less regressed ones from later periods of development: "a wish which is represented in a dream must be an infantile one" (154, 194, 253, and 592).[1]

Critics have frequently assumed that Freud thought all dreams were based on an infantile wish to have genital intercourse with the parent of the opposite sex. This is a grievous error. In the first place, Freud had in mind children of roughly ages two and a half to four, when the oral (nursing) and anal (toilet-training) periods of development are completed, and before the "latency period" (ages five to twelve) subordinates sexuality to the mastery of prevocational tasks. He knew that such small children's understanding of sexuality was quite different from adults'. And he believed that children's sexual feelings were not exclusively focused in the genitals, but rather diffused over the whole body. In the second place, when he says "sexual" he is referring to "libidinal" impulses in general rather than to specifically genital ones. He means physical gratification of all kinds—pleasurable impulses rather than destructive ones. In a footnote added to chapter 4 of *The Interpretation of Dreams* in 1925, Freud defends himself against the misrepresentation that psychoanalysis claims all dreams have a sexual content. He points out the great variety of wishes that are fulfilled in his examples of children's dreams: to take part in an excursion, go for a sail, make up for a missed meal, and so forth. He adds that he has provided other examples of dreams inspired by hunger, thirst, the need to relieve oneself, and by the desire to go on sleeping (194).

In its immediate context, Freud's protest seems plausible. But when we read accounts of how he traces free associations to his own or more particularly to patients' dreams in psychoanalysis, we cannot escape the impression that these associations lead almost invariably to a sexual core. There is an obvious reason, but Freud got in trouble for not spelling it out. Dreams that fulfill wishes for food, rest, or innocent recreation do not provoke conflicts in our mind. We do not consider such wishes immoral; we are not horrified at ourselves for having them. It is the sexual wishes above all that shock us, that put one part of our mind at war with another, that we are not willing to own—and that consequently conceal themselves within neurotic symptoms like a hermit crab in its borrowed shell. Therefore it is these sexual dreams that are of prime importance in therapy, whose purpose is to alleviate emotional suffering. Where Adler, Jung, and later analysts seem most justified in seeking to modify Freud's theories is in emphasizing our aggressive wishes as well as the sexual. For desires to hurt or kill another person, wishes for vindictive triumph or destruction are also repugnant to our conscience.

Moreover, Freud's disclaimer seems disingenuous in the context of the entire *Interpretation of Dreams*. Several hundred pages after the chapter 4 footnote, he identifies four different sources for the wishes that dreams may seek to gratify: (1) wishes generated by bodily needs during the night (e.g., dreams of eating and drinking); (2) wishes arising during the previous day that have not yet been fulfilled (e.g., going for a sail); (3) wishes that were denied and repressed during the previous day, being expelled from the preconscious into the unconscious; and (4) wishes imprisoned in the unconscious from the beginning and able to escape from it only in heavily disguised form. To defend himself against the charge that he finds all dreams sexual, he gives examples only from the two unrepressed classes, (1) and (2). So he evades the issue raised by his own opinion that repression is much more highly developed in adults than in children, and that no dream can be formed without the impetus provided by the repressed libido cathected by (stored in) the unconscious wish that—without the aid of psychotherapy—is permanently debarred from consciousness. For eventually he plainly says: "My supposition is that a conscious wish can only become a dream-instigator if it succeeds in awakening an unconscious wish with the same tenor [feeling tone] and in obtaining reinforcement from it [in adult dreams]." These unconscious wishes continually lie in wait for a weaker conscious wish on which they can ride piggyback, as it were, into our sleeping mind. On the surface it will look as though only the conscious wish had been realized in the dream; only some odd detail will point to the powerful unconscious source, of infantile origin. Freud admits that this hypothesis cannot always be proved, but he believes it often can—and that in any event it cannot be disproved (589–92).

Why Dream? Wish Fulfillment versus Anxiety

Only years later, in the *Introductory Lectures on Psycho-Analysis*, did Freud make it clear that although the repressed infantile wish is indispensable to the formation of the dream—our unconscious seeks only pleasure (Freud modified this view still later in *Beyond the Pleasure Principle*) and embarks on no project without the hope of receiving some gratification from it—that wish is not necessarily the key element of meaning for understanding the individual dreamer. The wish may be brought in as an attempt to reshape unpleasant thoughts; and indeed these thoughts may overwhelm the wishful impulse and abort the dream by transforming it into an anxiety dream from which the dreamer will try to escape by awakening. Dealing with the unpleasant thoughts will then become the major task of the analysis at that moment. In lecture 14 on "Wish-Fulfilment" Freud gives the example of a woman who has just heard that a friend has become engaged. She herself has been married for a long time; she feels jealous of her friend, whose fiancé seems more desirable than her own husband. In her dream she is at the theater with her husband. One side of the box stalls is completely empty, although her friend and her fiancé had wanted to go too but did not because no more good seats were left. In the dreamer's associations she recalled having been so eager to go to the theater the previous week that she had bought the tickets early and paid an agent's fee. This proved quite unnecessary because half the boxes were empty at the performance. Freud invokes two rules of interpretation: the dreamer's associations to a dream should be considered as part of the dream and analyzed along with it. Also, absurdity in a dream (good seats were unavailable beforehand; at show time half the good seats are empty) typically means that the dreamer is passing judgment on some situation she finds absurd. Freud concludes that the latent dream thought, the repressed disagreeable reaction, was "It was absurd to marry so early; I could have done much better had I waited." But Freud believes that the dreamer's curiosity about the possibility of a better marriage could not generate a dream by itself. To find expression, it had to awaken the old wish to find out what happened in marriage. Marriage was symbolized by going to the theater. The dreamer's present defeat was replaced by her earlier triumph, when she had been able to gratify her curiosity while her friend had had to wait (had been excluded from the theater— *Introductory Lectures*, 225; in *The Interpretation of Dreams*, see 450–52). In turn, Freud could have added, the triumph of marrying first harks back to the sexual curiosity of early childhood—to infantile voyeurism.

When Freud speaks of dream wishes he ordinarily means repressed ones generated by the sexual and aggressive impulses of the infantile id.[2] But in time, Freud came to realize that each part of the psyche—id, ego, and superego—may fulfill a wish in a dream. As we have seen, the ego feels the unrepressed wish to go on sleeping: it ingeniously weaves potentially disruptive external and internal stimuli into the ongoing dream narrative for as long as possible. Such "dreams of convenience" are the "guardians of sleep."[3] But the sadistic aspect of the superego (which must be distinguished from the beneficent aspect of conscience) may dramatize its own wishes for punishments that serve to alleviate the dreamer's guilt. Since such wishes lead to "unpleasure," which the organism strives always to avoid, Freud believes they could not provide the original indispensable motivating force for the dream, but they could enter into it once it was under way.

The full development of Freud's concept of the superego occurred twenty-three years later in *The Ego and the Id*. In *The Interpretation of Dreams* the concept appears in larval form as Freud struggles to explain unpleasant dreams without sacrificing the notion of wish fulfillment. In 1911 he added a discussion of what he at the time called "hypocritical" dreams. An example was his own recurring dream of working in a chemical laboratory. He had done so as a young doctor, but he felt he had no talent for precise experimental work. He remembered this period of his apprenticeship as sterile and humiliating (512–13). The word *analysis* links these dreams to the past. The psycho*analyses* of which he is proud in the present remind him of the less successful chemical *analyses* he performed early in his career. If dreams fulfill wishes, Freud wonders, why does this dream seem to take sides with self-criticism rather than with pride, and remind him of his humble beginnings in science as a warning not to form too exalted an opinion of himself? In 1919 he ventured the explanation that the mind contains "masochistic impulses" that might be gratified by a reversal of his present fame and achievement. He says he would be willing to identify a distinct class of "punishment dreams" as contrasted with "wish-fulfilment dreams." As the 1911 text picks up again, Freud retreats from this concession. He finds a way to salvage the idea that dreams fulfill wishes after all. For in his associations, during the gloomy year in the chemical lab and his lack of financial prospects, he discovered to his surprise that there were several women he could marry. So now in his mid-forties, Freud's unconscious wish that he and his wife could once again be young had made it possible for the conflict between vanity and self-criticism to appear as a dream (514). Freud finally resolved the issue more satisfactorily in a footnote added in 1930: "Since psycho-analysis has divided the personality into an ego and super-ego, it has become easy to recognize in these punishment dreams fulfilments of the wishes of the superego" (514).

THE PROBLEM OF ANXIETY DREAMS

If dreams are basically wish fulfillments as Freud claims, why do we remember so many of them as having been distressing? He deals with this issue relatively early in *The Interpretation of Dreams*. Wishes are always striving to be fulfilled in the dream's *latent* content—the meaning unearthed by psychoanalysis. The *manifest* content—what we remember—may show no trace of them. Our basic instinct of all instincts is to seek pleasure and avoid "unpleasure" (*Unlust*). In adults, the contents of the unconscious have always already been censored in the unconscious itself.[4] Therefore, giving free rein to the id in our dreams would produce affects (emotional reactions) that would have been originally pleasurable, but that would now be unpleasant owing to the condemnation by the censorship. We obviate the danger of such unpleasure by throttling or at least heavily disguising unconscious impulses. But if our repudiated wishes overcome the censorship and find direct or recognizable expression, then the censorship is replaced by anxiety. "Whereas we can say of an infantile dream that it is the open fulfilment of a permitted wish, and of an ordinary distorted dream that it is the disguised fulfilment [in the manifest content] of a repressed wish [from the latent content], the only formula that fits an anxiety-dream is that it is the open fulfilment of a repressed wish."[5]

Often enough in everyday life we experience fears, worries, and regrets. Since these feelings naturally form an important part of the day residue, they will be utilized by our dreams. If the dream-work succeeds in replacing all these unpleasurable affects with pleasant ones, we may achieve an undiluted wish-fulfillment dream. But more often than not, distressing memories from the previous day make their way as far as the manifest content of the dream. Sometimes, in the dream, we regard them with indifference; sometimes they provoke renewed discomfort; sometimes they make us so anxious on their own account that we awake. But in every case, the repressed wish that initiated the dream still tries to hitch a ride on the distressing affects. If the latent wish being fulfilled is gratifying enough, it cancels out the dream's unpleasant manifest content, which we can regard with indifference. But if the repressed wish breaks forth in too undisguised a form, the sleeping ego will feel vehement indignation and call an end to the dream with an "outburst of anxiety" (596).

Since a dream weaves its disguises from the day residue, the more unpleasant our recent waking impressions have been, the more effectively they can be employed to conceal unconscious wishes—you would be less likely to recognize a prince in beggar's rags than in a splendid robe. So it is precisely after those days when the dreamer has been sick, depressed, or both that the feeling tone carried over from waking provides the most propitious concealment for the inadmissible unconscious wishes. In addition, painful experiences during waking stir up hopes for better times, with which unconscious wishes can ally themselves (525). On the other hand, when the day residues have been unpleasant but have pointed to a forbidden gratification, then the superego (thus named by Freud only in a note added in 1930—earlier parts of the text call it the ego) may fulfill its own wishes, contrary to those of the id, by creating a "punishment dream" that reacts against the latent wish (597).

Why Dream? Wish Fulfillment versus Anxiety

What makes Freud so readable—and persuasive—is that he almost always illustrates and supports his theories with abundant examples. Twice *The Interpretation of Dreams* offers detailed discussions of how frustrating, unpleasant, or downright painful situations in dreams can conceal secret wishes (179–91 and 595–99). For Freud frankly admits that you never can take the wish-fulfilling function of disagreeable dreams for granted: you have to prove it by analysis every time (179). In his first example, a woman patient told the following dream: "I wanted to give a supper-party, but I had nothing in the house but a little smoked salmon. I thought I would go out and buy something, but remembered then that it was Sunday afternoon and all the shops would be shut. Next I tried to ring up some caterers, but the telephone was out of order. So I had to abandon my wish to give a supper-party" (180). As the dreamer produced associations, it turned out that on the previous day the woman's husband had decided that he had become overweight. He resolved to diet, exercise, and accept no more invitations to dinner.

Recently, he had also often made her jealous by praising one of her female friends. Fortunately that friend was thin, and the dreamer's husband preferred a full figure. The dreamer had visited her friend that same day. In the course of their conversation, which concerned the friend's wish to gain weight, the friend had inquired: "When are you going to ask us to another meal? You always feed one so well." On the surface, the dream of the thwarted supper party seemed to contain nothing but frustrations. The associations revealed that it actually gratified the dreamer's wish not to invite her friend, not to help her gain weight and thereby become even more attractive to her husband. The connection between dinner parties and gaining weight had been brought home to her by her conversations with her dieting husband the previous day. That there was only smoked salmon in the house was an allusion to the rival friend—it was her favorite food.

In another dream a young woman patient imagined that her sister's son Karl had died and was lying in his coffin. In real life, she had been strongly attracted to a man. It seemed that they might become engaged when suddenly her sister, acting in loco parentis, prevented the engagement for some unspecified reason. The man then no longer visited the sisters except once after a long absence when he returned to offer condolences after the sister's older boy Otto died. To imagine that Karl had died too represented the young woman's secret wish to see the man she had loved again when he would come once more to offer condolences to the family. Freud does not mention a possible secondary wish for a vindictive triumph: because the interfering sister had prevented her younger sibling from having the family that she wanted, then that sister would be punished by not having one either; she would lose her only remaining child.

A third dream was told to Freud by an acquaintance who wanted to prove that dreams do not always fulfill wishes: "I came up to my house with a lady on my arm. A closed carriage was standing in front of it and a man came up to me, showed me his credentials as a police officer and requested me to follow him. I asked him to allow me a little time to put my affairs in order" (188–89). The man had spent the night of the dream with a married woman with whom he was having an affair. The very first sentence contains a transparent disguise for the wish that they could be married. The man is bringing the lady home, as he could not in real life, and in German the verb used, *heim-führen*, means both "to take home" and "to marry." In real life the man tried to avoid making his lover pregnant because that would have given them away. He practiced coitus interruptus (withdrawing the penis before ejaculation). He feared that this time he had withdrawn too late. Then he slept and had his dream. In his associations to the dream, the crime he was accused of was infanticide. Thus he fulfilled his wish not to make his lover pregnant. His unconscious associated successful contraception with killing a baby because once in the past he had made a woman pregnant and she had had an abortion.

We must remember that no matter what else they do, in Freud's view dreams always fulfill the ego's wish to continue sleeping. At the same time they act as a safety valve that allows a regulated expression to the wishes of the id. So they are trying to juggle at least two potentially conflicting demands at the same time. If the wishful impulse becomes too overwhelming, if it threatens to achieve direct expression and thereby become recognizable in the dream, then the wish to continue sleeping will be sacrificed to the superego's wish to deny the existence of the unrestrained, amoral id. Then the dreamer will wake up in order to enlist the aid of the repressing powers of rational waking consciousness, which are stronger than our powers of repression during sleep (619). If we follow Freud's logic to its conclusion, we can speculate that when a superego punishment dream becomes too overwhelming, then the dreamer will also awake to escape the threat of death or dismemberment represented in the dream: insomnia is less undesirable than annihilation. In regard to dream wishes, any dreamer is like a composite of two separate people (620 n.). Any particular dream wish will be endorsed by only part of the dreamer's personality.

As Freud developed his theories over the years, the vexing problems raised by anxiety dreams did not go away. He was led to introduce more and more special explanations for them. He found that once his analysands had heard his theory that dreams fulfill wishes, they sometimes had dreams whose manifest content was markedly unpleasant, and which seemed motivated by the concealed wish to prove Freud's theory wrong. Some people had such dreams after merely hearing his lectures; and he predicts that some of us readers will have such dreams as well, so strong is our resistance to acknowledging our unconscious wishes (191–92).

A more widespread source of such "counterwish" dreams appears in certain people's masochistic tendencies. According to Freud, they have an aggressive, sadistic streak that has been transformed by reaction-formation. (Reaction-formation is a defense that consists in replacing an unacceptable feeling by its exaggerated contrary. Example: worrying about the safety of people whom you unconsciously wish dead.) Some find sexual gratification impossible unless physical pain is inflicted on them; others, the "mental masochists," crave humiliation and emotional abuse. Such people may have unpleasurable dreams that fulfill their wish for suffering. Freud gives the example of a young man who had a homosexual attachment to his brother. In earlier years he had concealed this attraction from himself by acting disagreeably toward his brother and tormenting him. Then he underwent a fundamental personality change and became submissive. He dreamed that his brother had sold the business that he himself looked forward to running one day. Here Freud sees a masochistic wish fulfillment: "It would serve me right if my brother were to confront me with this sale as a punishment for all the torments he had to put up with from me" (192–93).[6]

Years later Freud tried to stretch his theory concerning anxiety dreams to make it fit the recurring nightmares of the shell-shocked veterans of World War I, and of children who had been beaten or sexually abused. (Contrary to the opinion of many modern critics, Freud knew full well that such abuse occurred—see 218 n., e.g.) The brutal slaughter of the war forced Freud—along with nearly all Europeans—to recognize primordial destructive and self-destructive impulses in human beings. This horrifying realization crushed the optimism that had flourished during the era of peace, progress, and plenty extending from 1880 to 1914. Reactions were diverse: Catholic and Anglican religious revivals; radical assaults on bourgeois society (the Russian Revolution, dada, and surrealism), and Freud's postulation of a "death instinct" in *Beyond the Pleasure Principle* (1919). He speculated that the nightmares accompanying what we now call the posttraumatic stress syndrome were attempts to master the trauma after the fact "by developing the anxiety whose omission was the cause of the traumatic neurosis" (*SE* 18:32). Most psychotherapists today would agree that mastery is the central issue, but not in the way that Freud said: we feel anxious enough while we are being shot at or raped. So in the modern view, the recurring dreams represent failed attempts by the ego to master an overwhelming experience of helplessness.

In 1923 Freud again admitted that posttraumatic dreams were exceptions to the general rule that all dreams aim at wish fulfillment.[7] But ten years later still (1933), in the *New Introductory Lectures on Psycho-Analysis,* he reverted to his original views and provided two explanations. He now held that when distressing childhood experiences returned in dreams during psychoanalysis, they represented attempts by the dream-work to transform the unpleasant memories into fulfillments of the sexual and aggressive instinctual wishes originally stirred up by the trauma. But he distinguished such dreams from the anxiety dreams of traumatic neurosis, where the dream's invariable attempt to fulfill a wish was thwarted by a stronger unconscious force: fixation on the trauma. Thus the dream was prevented from achieving its aims, and sleep became something dreaded rather than desired (29 ff.).[8]

Overall, the history of Freud's theories regarding anxiety dreams shows him divided between two contradictory impulses. A guiding principle of scientific research is that, all other things being equal, the most "parsimonious" theory is best—the theory that is simplest, that requires the fewest explanations and exceptions. So for scientific reasons as well as for aesthetic ones (as a writer seeking a neat presentation), Freud had a vested interest in demonstrating that all dreams were basically wish fulfillments—at least, on the deepest, most infantile level. But at the same time, he was too honest and conscientious as a researcher not to grapple with observed cases that did not conform to his rules. If he had been able to benefit from the findings of modern dream research he would have known that night terrors, nightmares, and the recurring dreams of posttraumatic stress syndrome are biochemically distinct from the dreams he typically analyzed. If he had worked extensively with schizophrenics, he might have concluded that their lurid dreams of helplessness and dismemberment do not fulfill wishes, either. Had he participated in the extensive empirical studies of recent decades, involving frequent wakenings of subjects, he probably would have agreed that much mental activity during sleep is nothing more than banal, sterile musing on petty practical concerns of the previous day. His theories apply best to, and his examples all are drawn from, the vivid remembered dreams of ordinary and of neurotic (but not psychotic) people. But this is a minor limitation. His findings remain enormously fruitful. He was the first to map in detail the mental no-man's-land where the voluntary and involuntary meet. And without his pioneering research, how many of the subsequent studies of dreams would ever have been undertaken?

Part of Freud's collection of antiques. *Courtesy of Mary Evans / Sigmund Freud Copyrights.*

8

Dreams' Disguises

The most enduring contribution of *The Interpretation of Dreams* is its chapter 6, "The Dream Work" (311–546). It explains how the sleeping mind covers its tracks, how censorship forces inadmissible thoughts to make themselves unrecognizable before they can play a part in dreams. Freud's accounts of how the mind operates in producing dreams, jokes, and fantasies have opened up lines of investigation that are far from being exhausted a century later.[1]

The simplest, most effective disguise a dream can have is to be altogether forgotten once we have awakened. Freud sees our mental life in sleep as being like a riotous party of unbridled impulses that fall silent as soon as they come under the stern scrutiny of rational waking consciousness. He thinks the censorship makes us forget dreams. In other words, we forget dreams because we want to forget. But this view has become hard to sustain in the face of empirical research conducted since the discovery of REM sleep in the 1950s. Wakened during REM sleep, people can recall dreams nearly all the time. But the slightest distraction, such as having them call the weather number and record the temperature before writing down their dreams, will make them recall dreams only half as often. What makes us forget is what happens during the first moments of waking: the dreamer's mind is flooded with sense impressions. The fading dream, unlike most conscious thoughts, is unsupported by anything immediately present in the real world. So it cannot compete for our attention unless the dreamer "consolidates" it by immediately reflecting on it for at least a few seconds. This moves the dream from short-term into long-term memory.

Implicitly, according to Freud's understanding of the dream, at least three forces operate simultaneously during sleep. The id-impulse struggles to burst into consciousness; the censorship judges and condemns the impulse, blocking all its direct paths; the dream-work achieves a compromise between id and censorship by providing indirect pathways for the impulse. But this happens without premeditation. "[The dream-work] does not think, calculate or judge in any way at all; it restricts itself to giving things a new form" (545).

According to Freud, there is a three-stage pathway between repressed wishes and the manifest dream. First these wishes give rise to unconscious dream thoughts. To be able to sleep, the conscious self or ego has attempted to "decathect" (to neutralize) thoughts and feelings left over from the day. The unconscious resists this pressure. It recathects these thoughts and feelings as it allies itself with them. Either unconscious impulses have already become linked with waking impressions during the day, or have become linked to them in sleep owing to the lowering of the barriers between preconscious (forgotten but accessible) and unconscious (repressed and inaccessible). A preconscious dream wish takes shape. It finds a way to express the still deeper unconscious impulse by using the raw materials of the preconscious day residues. Then, still in the unconscious, the dream-work processes of "primary elaboration"—condensation, symbolization, and displacement—translate the preconscious wishes into images, into what the dreamer sees. We may never have been aware of this preconscious wish; it may be irrational, like anything unconscious that is translated into consciousness (226). So it is distinct from the wishful impulses that may have arisen during the day and which remain present among the preconscious dream thoughts, but it uses them for reinforcement whenever they are available. Dreams, like neurotic symptoms, result from a compromise between impulse and inhibition. The dream-work, Freud believes, may spend more than twenty-four hours seeking avenues for this compromise. Then the disguised dream wish is hallucinated, creating a temporary belief in the sleeper that it is being fulfilled.[2] Since the unconscious in and of itself does not distinguish between fantasy and reality, it finds just as much gratification in an imaginary fulfillment as it would in a real one. The dreamer's free associations are necessary to lead us behind the facade of the dream disguise to the preconscious dream wish, and then from that wish still deeper to the primordial, unconscious wish.

Depending on the context, Freud's term *manifest content* may refer to either the second or the final stage of the progression from unconscious wish to observable dream. For sometimes by *manifest content* he means what the dreamer sees; sometimes he means what the dreamer remembers; and sometimes he refers to the words the dreamer uses to report what she chooses to share from her memories. The first of these three aspects—the dream images—has been distorted by primary elaboration. Only the last aspect—the verbal dream report—is available for empirical scrutiny. But Freud knows that the dream is undergoing further distortion as it passes from vision to memory and from memory to report. Freud calls this further distortion "secondary elaboration." The dream pictures, often grotesque, disgusting, disjointed, or absurd, are transformed into a coherent narrative called the "dream facade" in order to satisfy the waking ego's sense of order and meaningfulness. Secondary elaboration also disguises any uncomfortable thoughts that the dreamer senses are coming too close to being disclosed despite primary elaboration—although she may not know precisely what they are. The more highly organized the verbal account of a dream, the more the original unconscious materials have been disguised. Unconscious irrationality has been plastered over with conscious rationality. Any ostensible continuity in a dream is suspect (538).

Freud also suggested an alternative explanation for certain exceptionally coherent dreams. He believed that our fantasy life often elaborated long stories ahead of time (i.e., before a given dream occurred) and that these could be activated and called up en bloc by the dream-work. In such cases our thought may be enormously accelerated. Freud cites a dream by the prominent nineteenth-century sleep researcher Maury. He had an elaborate dream of being led to the guillotine and executed, although the whole must have occurred during the instant after a piece of wood fell from his headboard and struck him on the neck (533–35). Freud thinks it quite possible that a physical stimulus to the dreamer simply activates such fantasies, and that they are remembered entire only once the dreamer awakes, when they are confused with the dream that alluded to them at one point or another.

Freud's views on secondary elaboration evolved. During the composition of *The Interpretation of Dreams* and for years afterward he sometimes spoke of it as if it were part of the dream-work. He then believed that our desire for intelligibility could influence our remembrance of a dream not only before we arrived at the manifest content (here meaning, presumably, the narrative constructed from the dream images), but even before we could perceive the dream at all. From 1923 on he adopted the more consistent position—since he said the dream-work has no judgmental or rational capacities—that secondary elaboration was a separate process peculiar to waking, a waking reaction to the memory of a dream. *The Ego and the Id* says that language is an ego function, and the way that unconscious contents become conscious, but that it has nothing to do with the way in which those contents are processed within the unconscious itself. The narrative coherence achieved by secondary elaboration is an artifact of waking.[3]

Nevertheless, Freud believed "interpreting means finding a hidden sense in something" (*SE* 15:87): the analyst's job was to trace back through the two layers of distortion—primary and secondary revision—to the original dream thoughts. This sounds as if primordial wishes were framed in a logically coherent, quasi-linguistic way; that the dream-work destroyed or reencoded this primordial coherence, or both; and that the psychoanalyst reestablished it. But, recent critics object, Freud's published examples provide no evidence of primordial coherence; they do not extract a kernel of significance. Instead, to the manifest dream, the patient's case history, and the associations, Freud adds another layer of complexity, namely the dream's interpretation. For instance, during the process of interpreting his "Dream of Irma's Injection" he finds connections between three different women in his mind: but he is not proving that the original latent dream thoughts were based on these connections. "First, the dream does not represent or express similarity, but creates it. Second, interpretation does not discover the point of comparison but makes it. And third, this logical connection must seem peculiarly illogical because it does not contain within itself the logic of the comparison."[4]

Such a caution is essential both because of Freud's loose, informal use of language and also because of the abuses of some of his followers who claim to be able to reduce every dream or fantasy to a straightforward psychoanalytical meaning. In fairness to Freud, however, we must add that he himself was not at all dogmatic or presumptuous regarding the powers of interpretation. In the first place, he lacked any positivistic faith in the ultimate precision of language. "Words," he said, "since they are the nodal points of numerous ideas, may be regarded as predestined to ambiguity" (376). He clearly said that a coherent and apparently complete interpretation always could overlook dimensions of a dream because each element of the dream is "overdetermined" by a multiplicity of converging meanings. Moreover, the results of our interpretations of our own dreams remain ultimately uncertain and unverifiable because the same instinctive censorship responsible for distorting a dream during its formation will also oppose itself to the act of interpretation (563). And even the best interpretations leave a core of mystery at "the dream's navel, the spot where it reaches down into the unknown. The dream-thoughts to which we are led by interpretation cannot, from the nature of things, have any definite endings; they are bound to branch out in every direction into the intricate network of our world of thought" (564).[5] Only if we keep Freud's prudent reservations in mind will we capture the flavor of his views concerning how dream-work encodes the latent content. He names four dominant shaping principles: considerations of represent-ability, condensation, displacement, and symbolization. But these are not recipes that can unlock all dreams; they are only guidelines.

CONSIDERATIONS OF REPRESENTABILITY

The limitations imposed by a basically nonverbal format are the main reason dreams often appear strange. As in the parlor game charades, the primary elaboration has to find ways of translating abstract ideas into visual impressions. For example, if you have to act out *The Sound and the Fury* you will need to communicate the general category (book title) and the key words. With gestures, you can suggest *sound* with a word that sounds alike—*round, pound, mound,* and so forth. But for *fury,* since the similarly sounding word *jury* is hard to suggest with pantomime, you will probably choose instead to mime the meaning—the emotion of extreme anger. Freud likens dream images to a rebus—a picture puzzle. Imagine a landscape with a boat on the roof of the house, a letter of the alphabet standing nearby, and a running headless man larger than the house. The picture is full of absurdities; what you must do is figure out what each separate element represents, and only then fit them together (312).

Freud gives an example of such a dream. A woman dreams she is watching a Wagner opera. Nearby her male cousin sits with his young wife, on the other side of whom is the aristocratic lover this wife has openly brought back from her honeymoon. The conductor runs about a high platform surrounded by an iron fence at the top of a tower as he directs the orchestra far below. She herself sits with a woman friend. To warm her unheated stall, her younger sister tries to hand her up a large glowing coal.

Freud reads this dream as a tissue of punning allusions to the dreamer's secret love for the musician Hugo Wolff, who had gone mad. She sees him as "towering above" other musicians, but also confined by the railing—like an animal (wolf) in a zoo or like a madman. The images of confinement and of the tower, taken together, evoke the German word *Narrenturm* or "fools' tower," an old word for "asylum." Shameless open love (her adulterous cousin who like her is associated with a "highly placed" beloved, the aristocrat) contrasts with her own secret devotion. Both she and the friend beside her have never married (in colloquial German, "have been left sitting"). Her younger sister, who still has marriage prospects, hands her a symbol of secret love, which the dreamer connects with the words of a German folksong: "No *fire*, no *coal* so hotly glows / As *secret love* of which no one knows" (377–79).

Considerations of representability pose more severe obstacles when the dream tries to represent logical relationships between two things or ideas: likeness, contrast, contradictions, wishes, doubts, hypotheses ("if . . . then . . ."), combinations, alternatives, cause and effect, repetition, closeness or remoteness in time or space, and so forth. To show a logical connection between things, dreams put them together in the same scene. For example, Freud tells a woman's dream where she first sees herself in a messy kitchen, scolding her servants for not having dinner ready. Then she imagines herself descending from a high place. Reversing the order of the two episodes, Freud interprets: "I wish I were of high descent (from a wealthy, powerful family). Because I am not, my life is sordid and unsatisfying" (350). Causality can also be suggested by having one thing change into another. But usually, Freud explains, dreams do not bother to represent it at all. Dreams can express "either-or" only by depicting both alternatives. (See the "Dream of Irma's Injection" examined in the next chapter.) But if a person *telling* a dream feels compelled to say "either-or" ("It was either a garden or a living room"), then the dream interpreter should assume that the referent has something to do with both (351–52).

"No" does not exist in dreams (353). But dreams can indicate a contradiction by reversing the ordinary situations of lived experience. So when an unknown young man attacked Freud's best friend Fliess in a book review, Freud dreamed that Germany's most famous writer, Goethe, was acting crazy in negatively reviewing an unknown young man. Freud thinks this dream means "just the opposite": it's the hostile critic, not the author being attacked, who is crazy and deservedly obscure (362).

Dreams can represent any situation by its wished-for contrary. Only the context and the dreamer's associations can clarify the issue. Ancient languages, Freud believes, reflected the primitive thinking of dreams. For example, in Latin *altus* means both "high" and "deep." *Sacer* means both "blessed" and "accursed."[6] "If a dream obstinately declines to reveal its meaning," Freud declares, "it is always worthwhile to see the effect of reversing some particular elements in its manifest content, after which the whole situation often becomes immediately clear" (363). So a dream may show a cause before the effect that it produces, or the conclusion to a line of reasoning before the premises that led to it. Freud closes his discussion of reversals with a compound illustration. A man dreamed his father was scolding him for coming home late. The dreamer's associations revealed the core meaning: he was angry at his father. (In the dream his father is angry at him.) He had been afraid of him, and always remembered that when he was a child he had been threatened by someone saying, "Just you wait until your father gets back." The dream conceals an infantile death wish against his father: the father always got home too early for the dreamer, and it would have been better if he had not come home at all (364).

Dreams may suggest similarity by using one person to represent two or several who share a trait in the dreamer's eyes. Sometimes the dream gives itself away by combining the name of one person with the features of another, or giving one person words or gestures characteristic of another. This combining process sometimes breaks down: then one of the persons being compared will simply be present without any apparent function ("my mother was there as well"). But often, too, an ostensible common element hides another, censored one. In the opera dream just discussed the unpleasant fact that "my friend and I both are too old to marry" is translated as the more tolerable "my friend and I are sitting together" with the puns on *sitzen geblieben* (remain sitting = on the sidelines = single) revealing the true point of comparison (354–57).

"If" may be suggested by interrupting the narrative progress of the dream: "but then it was as if I were somewhere else" (371). Recurrence is rendered by multiplying an object in question. A child of four who dreamed of eating one pear and longing for another was expressing the wish to suckle again at his mother's breast as in times past (407). When possible, dreams represent time by space; people who seem far off in dreams are meant to be remote in time. A bridge may stand for transitions or changes in condition. A hopeless wish may appear as a bridge too short to reach the opposite shore. Being paralyzed in a dream expresses an unresolved inner conflict. And two successive dreams may serve to disguise wish fulfillment. If one represents punishment and the second an illicit act, the two together may be saying that the dreamer can allow herself to do what is forbidden if she accepts the consequences. A person who is the object of an inadmissible desire may appear undisguised in a first dream, while the desired action will be represented directly in the second, in which the object has become unrecognizable or been replaced by someone indifferent.[7]

CONDENSATION

Several sources can and frequently do create one composite dream image, as we have just mentioned in the remarks on similarity.[8] Each element of the manifest content is "overdetermined": there are many different reasons for it to be there, because it represents many different things at once (318, 312–13). The manifest dream never is more extensive than the latent one.[9] Indeed, Freud goes so far as to claim that "the dream-work is under some kind of necessity to combine all the sources which have acted as stimuli for the dream into a single unity in the dream itself" (212) whenever it is possible to establish connections among them (261). The reader may object that many of the connecting strands of thought came up not during the dreaming but after it, during the analysis (314). But Freud believes that the new connections made while a patient associates depend on preexisting, "deeper-lying connecting paths." In effect, Freud obliterates any distinction between the unconscious associational network of the mind in general, and the associational network activated during the dream. His tacit assumption is that during dreams the entire contents of the unconscious are always potentially available to us. Since "free associations" can only reflect this preexisting structure, they can be no more creative than the dream-work is.

Freud illustrates condensation by referring to a dream scene intermediate between an attic, a bathhouse, and a changing room: it represents the attic where the dreamer undressed with other children in order to satisfy sexual curiosity (360). Another example is the dream of a young man who fears that marriage will cost him his freedom: he is arrested and led away to be questioned by a police inspector who turns out to be a woman with a child (532–33). In a more elaborate dream, an elderly woman has two may-beetles in a box. She realizes she must set them free before they suffocate. When she opens the box, one beetle flies out the open window. The other is crushed when she closes the window at someone's request. Among her numerous associations: she was born and married in May; she feels trapped in an unhappy marriage; the crushed beetle suggests the aphrodisiac cantharides ("Spanish fly") that her husband would need to make him more passionate. She is shocked at imagining herself angrily telling her husband "go hang yourself"; this thought again leads to thoughts of his disappointing lack of potency. Hanged men are supposed to have an erection and ejaculate as they die: the angry words are a way of saying "go get yourself an erection at any price!" Closing the open window not only suggests the marriage trap but also alludes to a major disagreement between the woman and her husband. She loves fresh air: he cannot stand it. And finally, the exhaustion of the beetles at the beginning reflects the patient's major physical complaint at the time of the dream.

Condensation is most obvious in the invented words and names that often appear in dreams. After Freud reads an article sent by a medical colleague, whose style he finds exaggerated and emotional, he dreams the sentence: "It's written in a positively *norekdal* style." According to Freud's free associations, the invented word suggests the German hyperboles *kolossal* and *pyramidal* (colossal; monumental)— praise that becomes sarcastic because it is so exaggerated—but also combines "Nora" and "Ekdal," protagonists from Ibsen's plays *A Doll's House* and *The Wild Duck*. The colleague in question had recently published a newspaper article on Ibsen; Freud's dream means that he finds his colleague's scientific article melodramatic and theatrical.

DISPLACEMENT

In condensation, one idea takes on itself the entire cathexis (unconscious emotional charge) of several others, creating a bizarre composite word or image that is sure to call attention to itself. Displacement is nearly the opposite: an idea surrenders its entire quota of cathexis to another so that it no longer attracts attention to itself at all.[10] The censorship imposes displacement on forbidden ideas during the primary process of unconscious dream construction. Either the repressed idea is replaced by another that merely alludes to the original, or else emphasis shifts from the essential element of a situation onto a secondary, unimportant aspect of it—or the feeling tone may change from serious to comical.[11] So "what is clearly the essence of the dream-thoughts need not be represented in the dream at all" (340). For instance, the dream of the may-beetles focuses entirely on the insects, but the associations to the dream reveal that its true topic is the relationship between sexuality, anger, and cruelty. The chain of associations runs "crushed beetle—aphrodisiac—violent means to make a man have an erection—anger—sexual frustration."

To invoke displacement may seem to invite gratuitous and farfetched speculation. Obviously the concept could be seriously misused. But Freud proposes from everyday life a host of related examples that we take for granted: "When a lonely old maid transfers her affection to animals, or a bachelor becomes an enthusiastic collector, when a soldier defends a scrap of colored cloth—a flag—with his life's blood, when a few seconds' extra pressure in a handshake means bliss to a lover, or when, in *Othello,* a lost handkerchief precipitates an outburst of [murderous] rage—all these are instances of psychical displacements to which we raise no objection" (210). Actually, the first two examples illustrate sublimation (replacing one goal with another) and the third (the flag) illustrates universal symbolism. Displacement in the strict sense is illustrated by only the last two of the five. Symbolism that is not arbitrary and conventional like the flag relies upon a perceived similarity between two objects that may hardly ever appear together (e.g., snake/penis). Displacement shifts from one thing to another that may not resemble the first but that tends to occur near it in time or space (e.g., handshake/embrace; woman's handkerchief/woman's body).

Trivial impressions from the distant past (like "screen memories" from childhood) may find their way into our dreams if they have already been cathected by a displacement in that distant past. From then on they retain the importance that originally belonged to the idea from which our emotional focus was shifted: therefore they do not quickly fade as ordinary insignificant impressions would. No dreams are innocent; "nothing that has *really* remained indifferent can be reproduced in a dream" (215).

The simplest examples of displacement are numbers in dreams. The number is significant but its referent changes to something inconsequential. Time of day in a dream may refer to the dreamer's age in childhood; a woman dreaming of walking with two little girls fifteen months apart in age alludes to two traumatic events fifteen months apart in her own childhood (444); a dangerous flood of thirty-degree water may suggest a person's fears of being suddenly frozen with old age upon turning thirty. Dreams within dreams are a special case of partially unsuccessful displacement. The main dream attempts to replace the inner dream, whose significance is denied because it is represented as "just a dream." That is a clue to its special importance.[12]

SYMBOLIZATION

This section (385–439) presents the most misused portion of Freud's theories on dream-work. The temptation for lazy analysts and critics is to go through a dream, fiction, fantasy, or emotionally charged situation without exploring the history and associations of the person who is fantasizing, but merely saying A = B: "This is your father, and that is your mother; this is a penis, and that is a vagina; this is castration, and that is masturbation." But no recipe always works, and nothing can replace alert give-and-take with a living patient. Freud intended symbolic interpretation to serve only as an adjunct to free association when the patient produced few or no associations to the dream (274 n.). Without interviewing the patient, you never can tell for sure whether a given symbol is personal or conventional in its meaning; you cannot tell which parts of the dream should be interpreted symbolically and which literally; and no dream will lend itself in its entirety to a symbolic interpretation. Associations are indispensable.[13]

To identify universal symbols, Freud drew widely from folklore, proverbs, jokes, songs, literature, and the fine arts. The history of his views on symbolization is complex. Under the influence of his fellow Viennese analyst Wilhelm Stekel, which reached its peak around 1909, Freud gave an increasingly important role to universal symbols in the interpretation of dreams. As early as 1911 Freud began to have doubts; he claimed that Stekel might have hurt psychoanalysis as much as he had helped it, by encouraging reductive, mechanical, or farfetched interpretations. In 1914 he condemned "the reckless interpretations of Stekel" (388). But he himself continued to add long lists of additional symbols to *The Interpretation of Dreams*, not only in 1909 but also in 1911, 1914, and 1919. In the 1914 edition for the first time he devoted a special titled section to dream symbolism. And in 1915 he gathered and synthesized his years of clinical observations of dream symbols in the widely read, influential tenth lecture in the *Introductory Lectures on Psycho-Analysis*. To the end, moreover, Freud acknowledged that Stekel had taught him much about universal symbolism.[14] With Freud's repeated cautions against merely translating symbols in mind, we can survey his identification of widespread and instinctive symbolism.

Birth. Freud finds that many dreams of being in water or going through narrow passageways are fantasies of being in the womb and being born. The dreamer often feels anxiety (435). For a woman, a dream of rescuing someone and especially of pulling someone from the water may refer to giving birth (439; the best-known example is the story of Moses found in the bulrushes). A woman's dream of losing a tooth (separation from a body part) can have the same meaning (423 n.). If you imagine death as a return to the womb, a bridge can represent the passage into the world or out of it. And "the legend of the labyrinth [Theseus and the Minotaur] can be recognized as a representation of anal birth. The twisting paths are the bowels and Ariadne's thread is the umbilical cord."[15] One could find a similar fantasy in Dante's journey through and out of Hell in the *Inferno*.

The Parents. These figures may appear in dreams as robbers or burglars (the father) or as ghosts (the mother in a pale nightgown). Such images derive from infancy when the parents entered the child's room to check on him or her during the night (439). In general a king or queen stands for the parents; famous men may signify the father (389).

The Self. This figure can be represented as a prince or princess (389). Freud believes that dreams without exception are completely narcissistic. (By this he does not mean devoid of altruistic impulses, but rather, centered on the self and its feelings, 304 n.) So if the dreamer does not appear as a character in a dream, she must be concealed behind another character with whom she has something in common. Even when the self does recognizably appear, others in the dream may represent the self as well, so that the ego appears several times over. Freud says we should no more be surprised at this than we are at everyday language where, for example, a sentence may include two selves: "When I [present self] think what I [past self] was like then . . ." (358). Wild beasts may dramatize some impulse the dreamer fears, or the libido (instinctual desire) in general. The dreamer's neurosis or psychosis may appear as a separate person (445). Elsewhere

Freud later observed that the devil may symbolize the repressed instinctual life.[16]

Childhood. This period may be suggested by depicting other people in the dream as enormous—as they were once seen by the child—or else at a great distance (replacing time with space, 443). Small animals and vermin may stand for small children such as unwanted brothers or sisters. A dream of being plagued with vermin may be a dream of pregnancy (392).

Excretion. This childish pleasure we have been forced to renounce may be recalled in a disguised form in dreams of joyous swimming or of fire (430). In the unconscious, fire often appears closely associated with the stream of urine that can extinguish it. Male urination may also connote ambition (seeing how far you can squirt). Semen may be disguised as urine or tears. Excrement can be represented by gold because of the high value a child may place on its feces, and its reluctance to part with them during the toilet-training phase (439). Toilet training may also teach the child that the feces are a treasured gift to the parents. A fascination with money (little hard bits of something stored up) may be related to the feces; a baby can also be associated with them through an unconscious revival of the infantile sexual theory that babies are born through the bowel. Finally, feces in the bowel may also stand for a penis, in remembrance of the pleasurable anal sensations of defecation that can dominate an infant's experience before the development of genital sexuality.[17]

The Female Sexual Organs. These can be symbolized by flowers or gardens—flowers are the sexual organs of plants—although a flower on an erect stalk may also betoken a penis (410–12). Hollow objects of all kinds can suggest the vagina or the womb—boxes, chests, luggage, containers, ships, rooms, caves, valleys, the mouth, and the ear; the vagina in particular may appear in the form of an enclosure, including walled cities and fortresses, and also as a doorway, gateway, and the like (355–59). Wood in general often seems to stand for women (391), perhaps because it is regularly penetrated (nailed, screwed, drilled) whenever we build things. But tables in particular have this association (390) because of our primordial experience of nursing = eating: witness the male proclivity for directing offensive sexual remarks at waitresses as opposed to saleswomen, policewomen, etc. Particularly in women, the pubic hair may be symbolized by moss, fur, velvet, forests. The spider mysteriously spinning threads drawn out of its own abdomen evokes the mother "so that the fear of spiders expresses dread of mother-incest and horror of the female genitals."[18]

The Penis. This organ appears in the form of elongated objects like sticks, canes, and poles; bodily appendages such as the nose, hands, or feet; neckties or hats (suggesting the enlarged glans at the end of the penis); sharp, penetrating weapons and tools such as drills and swords; tools and all sorts of complicated machinery and apparatus in general; tubes that can shoot, squirt, or give off smoke, such as firearms, cigarettes (a current ad campaign for one brand, mainly in women's magazines, is based entirely on the premise that longer is better), cigars, hoses, Roman candles, fountain pens, and the like; long flexible articles like whips, and animals such as snakes and lizards; mice and other small animals that go into holes; items that can expand, like balloons and umbrellas; things that rise, like dirigibles and planes. A classic modern example is Luke Skywalker's light-saber in *Star Wars*; in some posters he holds it near his crotch. In 1911 Freud associated dreams of flying with a male erection (430). The number three may connote the penis and testicles together, while any small round objects may connote the testicles. Smooth walls or facades suggest the male body; projections suggest the female. "Little ones" (children) can stand for the genitals in general.

Masturbation. This activity in males can be represented in dreams by losing a tooth or by pulling off something; in both sexes, by any regular hand movement that creates friction, such as rubbing or polishing. Also, by picking at something or fiddling with it, and by activities involving rapid movement of the fingers, such as playing a musical instrument or typing. Playing with or beating a small child also can symbolize masturbation (392).

Sexual Intercourse. From the male viewpoint intercourse can be represented by military victories, particularly by the conquering of a walled city or fortress. The military/erotic metaphor, of course, is a commonplace. A perfume manufacturer recently exploited this universal symbolism by naming a fragrance, "Chamade," a French word for the signal that besieged persons make with drums and trumpets when they want to surrender. For a woman, being run over by a vehicle or covered by something like a hat and overcoat can suggest intercourse (Freud scants the woman's viewpoint). For both sexes, intercourse can be represented by the act of mounting steps, staircases, and ladders: "mount" (*steigen*) evokes the sexual act in animals; the rhythmical movement accompanied by increasing breathlessness as you climb a stair corresponds to the sensation of coitus. Finally, "in dreams sweet things . . . stand regularly for caresses or sexual gratifications."[19]

Castration. The word means to cut off the testicles, to geld (as with horses and eunuchs). But Freud uses it to mean "cutting off the penis," so we must follow this misleading terminology here. So long as neurosis keeps most of our mental contents unconscious, in the world of id and superego there is no enjoyment without an equal and opposite reaction. This reaction is the superego threat, guilt and anxiety. Freud feels the main threat is "castration" (loss of the penis). He believes that little girls and boys both experience a shock when they discover that women have no penises. Girls then feel deprivation and "penis envy"; boys may develop a morbid fear of castration. Such a theory may seem farfetched today; it was much less so in middle-class European families at the turn of the century. Parents did not hesitate to discourage masturbation by telling little boys that unless they stopped it at once, their penis would be cut off. Freud in his case history of "Little Hans" thinks it routine that his mother would threaten to snip off his "widdler";[20] milder threats, also commonplace, were that the masturbator would get tuberculosis or go insane. Castration, Freud believed, might be depicted in a dream by a tooth being pulled, losing one's hair or having it cut (as in the legend of Samson and Delilah), or by being beheaded. "If one of the ordinary symbols for a penis occurs in a dream doubled or multiplied, it is to be regarded as a warding-off of castration" (392, 422 n.). In waking life, people who need many missiles or guns before they can feel secure are motivated by the same unreasoning, unconscious fear.

Psychoanalysis. Frequently analysis was represented in the dreams of Freud's patients by a journey, usually by automobile, since (Freud wrote in 1919) it was a modern, complicated vehicle. To make ironic allusions to the progress of the treatment, the patients might imagine the vehicle as excessively slow or in need of repair. In analysis dreams, subterranean regions such as caves and cellars may stand not for the womb, but rather for the unconscious (445).

Death. Dead people who appear in dreams may represent the thought: "If he or she were alive today, what would he or she think about what I am doing now?" If the sleeper feels that the situation is absurd, her reaction reflects the consoling thought that the dead person no longer can disapprove or interfere. If a figure in a dream alternates between being alive and being dead, the dream may be seeking a wished-for indifference ("I don't care whether that person is alive or dead") to replace the painful ambivalence that often haunts our attitude toward loved ones. If the dream itself makes no explicit reference to the fact that a character in it is actually dead, the dreamer may be thinking of her own death, represented by an implicit comparison to those with whom she finds herself (465–67). The death of the dreamer ordinarily stands for something else, such as going insane, while the actual threat of dying will be represented by the dream death of another person or animal. A wooden house or boat may represent not a womb, but a coffin (491–92). As in everyday speech, death can also be rendered by a scene of departing on a journey ("passing on"), crossing a bridge, or going through a hallway or passage (372 n., 420, 466–67, 489–91, 502, 510, and 515).²¹ Such actions, however, often have a different meaning: in many dreams the last segment of the manifest content represents the intention to awake or the process of awakening, which can be depicted by such images as crossing a threshold, passing from one room to another, departing, returning home, diving into water, and so forth (543).

Here is an example of Freud's symbolic interpretation of an entire dream as reported to him by another analyst. His comments have been removed from the footnotes and inserted into the main text in brackets.

> Then someone broke into the house and she was frightened and called out for a policeman. But he had quietly gone into a church [= vagina], to which a number of steps [symbol of copulation] led up, accompanied by two tramps. Behind the church there was a hill [*mons veneris*] and above it a thick wood [pubic hair]. The policeman was dressed in a helmet, brass collar and cloak [according to an expert, demons in cloaks and hoods are of a phallic character]. He had a brown beard. The two tramps, who went along peaceably with the policeman, had sack-like aprons tied around their middles [the two halves of the scrotum]. In front of the church a path led up to the hill; on both sides of it there grew grass and brushwood, which became thicker and thicker and, at the top of the hill, turned into a regular wood. (401–2)

Among the areas that Freud obviously neglected were clitoris symbolism, breast symbolism, and the symbolic meanings of colors in dreams. The clitoris may be suggested by a little knob or protuberance above the middle of something—particularly above an opening such as a fireplace or oven; or by a bird's beak.²² Breasts may be depicted as hills, curved surfaces, or fountains, and particularly by fruits— round objects that offer sweet nourishment (compare the well-known bon mot about an actress in a gold dress: "There's hills in them thar gold").²³ As for color, many people dream in it, despite occasional claims to the contrary. But as in real life, it tends to be overlooked in dreaming. When a color appears in a dream report it reveals a point of special emotional intensity; it highlights a detail and—in analysis—calls it to the therapist's attention. Color, a recent analyst observes, is the ego's way of flagging previously repressed material that is just beginning to emerge in the analysis, and which still is fraught with tension and risk.[24] In general, color may suggest the parts of the body that stand out visually from the rest because they are darker: lips, nipples, genitals, and the surrounding pubic hair. Finally, our childhood training to be clean and decent makes us keenly aware of stains that betray aggression, elimination, or ejaculation in an inappropriate place—red for blood, brown for feces, yellow for urine, white for milk or semen may be easily disguised in dreams by attributing these colors to an innocent-appearing object.

In 1911 Freud concluded that any group of ideas could stand for sexual facts and wishes (406). But elsewhere he protests that "the assertion that all dreams require a sexual interpretation, against which critics rage so incessantly, occurs nowhere in my *Interpretation of Dreams*. It is not to be found in any of the numerous editions of this book and is in obvious contradiction to other views expressed in it" (432; cp. 194 n.). The foregoing list of examples should bear out Freud sufficiently; by no means are all "Freudian symbols" sexual symbols. We should further recall Freud's conviction that no symbolic interpretation will be any more than an idle game unless it occurs in a secondary role and in the context of an analysis where the patient's history and associations are continuously brought into play. Even when a symbol is identified correctly, that identification in no way explains the dream as Freud understands it: a specific mental act that fits into the dreamer's current preoccupations in a precise, meaningful way.

9

"The Specimen
Dream of
Psychoanalysis"

Freud's *Interpretation of Dreams* begins by reviewing the previous
literature on the subject; then his short second chapter illustrates his
new method of interpreting by using the dreamer's associations; and
the last five chapters explore the theoretical implications of Freud's
ideas. His exhaustively interpreted dream in the second chapter is a
personal one. He called it "The Specimen Dream of Psychoanalysis,"[1]
but it is more commonly known as "The Dream of Irma's Injection."
Freud's analysis of it has provoked more reactions than any other part
of his book.

As usual, Freud tries to justify his method of interpretation from
the outset by showing the problems that arise from the existing methods for interpreting dreams. He agrees with the lay people who, unlike
the skeptical scientists of Freud's day, have always tended to take
dreams seriously and to find guidance in them. They have used one of
two methods. Some try to treat dreams as symbolic equivalents of real-
life situations. For example, in the Old Testament Joseph explains that
Pharaoh's dream of seven fat cows devoured by seven thin cows means
that seven years of plenty will be followed by seven years of famine.
So Pharaoh should store as much of the surplus harvest as possible to

prepare for the lean years. People believe that success in interpreting such dreams depends on the interpreter's intuitive sense of a higher order reflected in the dream. Alternatively, people attempt to interpret dreams item by item with the aid of a codebook. Unlike the first method of seeking an overall analogy, this second method can be effective in dealing with confused or incoherent dreams. The most noteworthy practitioner of the piecemeal method, Freud claims—and most scholars of the history of dream interpretation would agree with him today—was the second-century professional dream interpreter Artemidorus Daldianus. He wrote the *Oneirocritica*, a work consisting of a very detailed dream dictionary giving the meanings of individual images. Artemidorus's work has three great merits: it is quite complete; it acknowledges that the meaning of any particular symbol may vary according to the personal circumstances of the dreamer; and it explores the use of wordplay in dreams. A famous example of the last told by Artemidorus concerns the conqueror Alexander the Great. He had laid siege to the city of Tyre, but was beginning to wonder whether he could capture it. Then he dreamed of a satyr dancing on his shield. His companion Aristander interpreted the dream by breaking the Greek word for satyr, *satyros*, into two parts, *sa Tyros*, meaning "Tyre is thine." Encouraged, Alexander continued the siege and eventually took the city.[2]

In two essential respects, Freud's technique differs from that of the ancient interpreters like Artemidorus. Freud focuses on what occurs to the dreamer—not to the interpreter—as he or she looks over the dream. And this dreamer does not draw upon a preestablished list of correspondences between dream images and meanings. Freud begins by asking the dreamer to relate his or her dream, and then asks for personal associations to each detail of it. The dreamer is pledged to communicate everything that occurs to him or her without trying to judge it and censor it rationally or morally, even if his or her associations seem insignificant, senseless, or repellent. These "free" associations are unedited thoughts that arise when the mind is allowed to wander. Suspending rational control aims to make the patient's ideas more susceptible to the influences of unconscious material.

"The Specimen Dream of Psychoanalysis"

Free association is not a new idea. The French Renaissance philosopher Michel de Montaigne said that he let his mind run free while writing his *Essais*. But his avowed purpose is almost the opposite of Freud's: to have his mind learn discipline by contemplating and becoming ashamed of the disorderly products of its imagination. Freud wants us instead to acknowledge—not disavow—these products so as to rob them of the compelling power lent to them by repression.

Dream interpretation through associations undeniably provides a valuable therapeutic tool. Freud's sample "Dream of Irma's Injection" demonstrates the enormous richness of insight that can be achieved through adding associations to the manifest dream. This dream stands out among the others in Freud's book because in general he uses them only to make one particular theoretical point or to provide one specific kind of example. To find a full analysis of a dream in a therapeutic context, one must wait for his later case histories. But for this dream he offers sixteen pages of comments and associations (138–54).

In the summer of 1895 Freud had been psychoanalyzing a young woman friend of the family who suffered from hysterical anxiety and accompanying physical symptoms. The treatment had relieved the anxiety but not the other symptoms. Freud suggested an interpretation of her problem that the patient was unwilling to accept. At this impasse the partially successful treatment was interrupted for the summer holidays. Freud then met a junior colleague, "Otto," who had just seen "Irma" at her summer resort. Freud asked after her; Otto said she was better, but not quite well. Freud sensed a reproach in this reply. He felt annoyed, and in order to justify himself, that evening he wrote out an account of Irma's case to show to "Dr. M.," a mutual friend of his and Otto's. That night he had this dream:

DREAM OF JULY 23rd–24th, 1895

[1] A large hall—numerous guests, whom we were receiving.—Among them was Irma. I at once took her on one side, as though to answer her letter and to reproach her for not having accepted my 'solution' yet. I said to her: [2] "If you still get pains, it's really only your fault." She replied: "If you only knew what pains I've got now

in my [3] throat and stomach and abdomen—it's choking me"—I was alarmed and looked at her. She looked pale and puffy. [4] I thought to myself that after all I must be missing some organic trouble. [5] I took her to the window and looked down her throat, and she showed signs of recalcitrance, like women with artificial dentures. I thought to myself that there was really no need for her to do that.—She then opened her mouth properly and on the right [6] I found a big white patch; at another place I saw extensive whitish grey scabs upon some remarkable curly structures which were evidently modelled on the turbinal bones of the nose.—[7] I at once called in Dr. M., and he repeated the examination and confirmed it. . . . Dr. M. looked quite different from usual; [8] he was very pale, he walked with a limp and his chin was clean-shaven. . . . [9] My friend Otto was now standing beside her as well, and my friend Leopold was percussing her through her bodice and saying: "She has a dull area low down on the left." He also indicated that [10] a portion of the skin on the left shoulder was infiltrated. (I noticed this, just as he did, [11] in spite of her dress.) . . . M. said: [12] "There's no doubt it's an infection, but [13] no matter: [14] dysentery will supervene and the toxin will be eliminated." . . . [15] We were directly aware, too, of the origin of her infection. Not long before, when she was feeling unwell, [16] my friend Otto had given her an injection of a preparation of [17] propyl, propyls . . . propionic acid . . . [18] trimethylamin (and I saw before me the formula for this printed in heavy type.) . . . [19] Injections of that sort ought not to be made so thoughtlessly. . . . [20] And probably the syringe had not been clean.

Numbers inserted into the text above correspond to the detailed interpretations by Freud summarized below. My comments below are placed within parentheses.

(1) Day residue. Freud's wife has just told him that she expected a number of guests, including Irma, for her birthday. The dream anticipates this gathering. (2) At this time, Freud later admitted, he still thought of therapy as an intellectual process. He felt that once he had pointed out the unconscious causes of a patient's symptoms, the patient was responsible for accepting the explanation and getting well. He did not yet realize the necessity of the long process of "working through," during which the patient's resistance to understanding and

relinquishing the neurotic symptom (which has its own perverse satisfactions) gradually gives way first to an intellectual understanding, then in time to emotional acceptance, and later still, to changes in attitudes and behavior. (3) The real Irma complained of feelings of nausea and disgust, but had no symptoms in the throat or abdomen; moreover, she always had a rosy complexion. Freud begins to suspect that in the dream she stands for someone else. (4) Freud finds himself wishing that the doctor to whom Irma had originally gone for her physical complaints had overlooked an organic illness. Then that other doctor, not Freud, would be responsible for her not getting well. *He* was supposed to deal only with the emotional problem. (5) Freud's associations now lead him to recognize that Irma represents at least three other women in addition to herself: an attractive governess who tried to conceal her dental plates from Freud during a medical examination; an intimate friend of Irma's to whom Freud was attracted— she suffered from hysterical choking, had been diagnosed by Doctor M. as having a diphtherialike membrane of mucus in her throat, and had become Freud's patient in his fantasies, although in reality she managed to deal with her symptoms by herself; and Freud's wife, who was "bashful" in his presence and who would not have made "an amenable patient." (Although in good health, she had looked "pale and puffy" recently during her sixth pregnancy—a detail Freud alludes to and associates with a time when he had noticed her "bashfulness.") In a note here, Freud feels that the comparison of the three women (actually there are four, but apparently he wants to suppress one of them) conceals a deeper meaning that he will not explore because the resulting discussion would lead him "far afield." And he introduces his famous comment that at least one spot in every dream, it is "unplumbable" (143).

(6) Freud associates the ailing throat with Irma's friend's irritated throat; with the alarming illness (diphtheria) his eldest daughter had had two years before; and with his own troublesome nasal swellings, which he had tried to relieve by taking cocaine. He then feels guilt because he had recently learned that a woman patient of his who had taken cocaine for the same reason had extensively damaged her

mucous membrane, and because after Freud had published a paper recommending the therapeutic use of cocaine eleven years earlier, a good friend of his had become an addict and died. (7) He recalls that when a patient of his had died from another drug that Freud had prescribed because it was considered safe, he turned to Dr. M. for vindication. Freud's eldest daughter had the same name as this patient. He now felt that her diphtheria had seemed a punishment for his medical incompetence, and that his dream was trying to humiliate him by accumulating as many examples of this incompetence as possible. (8) The pallor corresponds to Dr. M.'s unhealthy appearance in real life, but his limping and being clean-shaven are features of Freud's older brother. He realizes that because he is irritated at both men for having turned down a suggestion he made to them, he has conflated them (combined them into one; here again Freud withholds personal information, perhaps concerning his finances). (9) Otto and Leopold had been Freud's assistants when he worked at the children's hospital. Otto was quick; Leopold was slow but sure. Freud feels he is criticizing Otto through an implicit comparison with the more careful Leopold. He also associates this pair of physicians with the "disobedient" Irma and her "wiser" friend, whom he preferred. (10) Refers to rheumatism in Freud's own shoulder. (11) In 1900 adult female patients did not undress in front of male doctors. Freud explicitly refuses to analyze any further the notion of seeing through a dress. (12) Freud feels the opinion is ridiculous but it reminds him of medical discussions during his daughter's illness. (13) "No matter" seems intended to console Freud and relieve him of guilt feelings not only for not having completely cured the real-life Irma, but also for having fantasized that she had a severe physical illness in order to clear himself in the dream. (14) Recently Freud had recognized that hysteria was the basis for a young male patient's constipation. Since he was unwilling to treat the man in psychotherapy he sent him on a sea voyage. From Egypt, where he had come down with dysentery, the rejected patient sent Freud a despairing letter. Freud felt the ignorant local practitioners had missed the true underlying cause of the dysentery, hysteria. But if the young man had contracted a real physical illness, Freud would have felt responsible. (12–14) are intended to make fun of Dr. M. *He* has Irma's desirable friend as a patient, but he probably thinks she has genuine tuberculosis and does not recognize her hysteria. Moreover, Dr. M. had irritated Freud by not believing his explanation of Irma's symptoms any more than Irma had herself.

(15) The dream's vested interest in blaming Otto is revealed by the illogic of Freud and his colleagues knowing the origin of an infection that has just that instant been discovered (by Leopold). (16) While staying with Irma's family recently, Otto had given an injection to a person in a neighboring hotel. Freud recalls that his friend who died had injected cocaine against Freud's advice, rather than taking it orally. (17) Otto had recently given the Freuds a bottle of liqueur that smelled so bad they threw it out. That smell reminds Freud of the chemicals named. (18) Freud recalls a conversation with his then best friend Wilhelm Fliess, who told him that one of the products of sexual metabolism was trimethylamin. The idea of the injection with a "sexual chemical" (suggesting intercourse with the ejaculation of sperm— but Freud is too delicate to say so) reminds Freud that both Irma and her friend are young widows. He hints that if they are ill (Irma despite psychoanalytic treatment) it is because their systems are poisoned by sexual deprivation. Fliess had speculated on a connection between the turbinal bones in the nose (observed in Irma's throat earlier in the dream) and the female sex organs. (19) Freud feels that Otto acted thoughtlessly and was too easily influenced in doubting the efficacy of Freud's treatment of Irma. He again feels guilt over the deaths of the friend and the patient mentioned in (6) above. (20) In contrast to "Otto's" carelessness, Freud asserts his own conscientiousness. For two years he has given injections twice a day to an old woman, and the syringe has always been clean. When this woman went on vacation she came down with an inflammation that Freud suspected came from a dirty syringe used by another doctor who was continuing the course of injections. This inflammation again reminds Freud of his wife, who had a similar complaint during pregnancy. "Though it will be understood that I have not reported everything that occurred to me during the process of interpretation" (151 n. [1909 edition]), Freud now

announces that he has completed the interpretation of the dream.

Freud then summarizes and develops his interpretation. The dream takes revenge on Otto for having given the family a disappointing present (the bottle of evil-smelling liqueur); more important, it throws back at Otto (what Freud felt to be) the latter's implied accusation of medical incompetence the previous day. The dream makes Otto rather than Freud responsible for Irma's continuing illness; then it adduces a whole series of other factors that also excuse Freud. The dream is motivated by a wish to escape blame. Its many associations can be grouped under the general heading of professional conscientiousness.

The dream struggles so hard to vindicate Freud, he admits, that it undermines itself: it offers so many lines of defense that they contradict each other. The four successive scenes are saying: "It's not my fault that she's still sick. She's not well *either* because she willfully refuses to accept my interpretation of her problem, *or* because she's sexually frustrated, *or* because she suffers from an organic disorder rather than the mental disorder I'm treating, *or* because my colleague was careless." Freud makes an amusing comparison to the protestations of a man accused of having damaged a kettle that he borrowed. "It wasn't damaged when I returned it. . . . It already had a hole in it when I borrowed it. . . . I never borrowed it at all" (153). The dream's methods are incoherent, but its purpose is coherent. It is trying to make a wish come true.

A great deal can be added to Freud's interpretation. Most important, the wish referred to here—to be exculpated—derives from the very recent past. It has been only lightly repressed into the preconscious. It is neither unconscious nor infantile, as the basic dream-motivating wishes in Freud's theory are supposed to be. Reading between the lines and noticing the dream-text details where Freud looks down a woman's throat (= vagina?) and sees through her dress, one might recognize the unconscious wish called scopophilia, the child's irrepressible sexual curiosity that leads her or him to try to spy out things that ordinarily are hidden. In the adult such curiosity is called voyeurism ("Peeping Tom" behavior). It can be sublimated by practicing psychoanalysis, one of the best ways of learning people's secrets.[3] In the male child, such curiosity was directed primarily toward the mother in the beginning, in turn provoking a sense of rivalry with and fear of retaliation from the father. In Freud's adult life the parent-imagos (fantasized images of the parents preserved in the unconscious) would have been reactivated by sexual frustration combined with contacts with female patients, and by feelings of rivalry with his male professional colleagues. In the unconscious, Freud's ambition at the time (1895) to cure hysteria more effectively than any of his colleagues could is equivalent to claiming that he could take care of his mother better than his father could. When Irma's persisting physical symptoms cast doubt on the success of this ambition, Freud underwent a crisis that is reflected in the dream. The dream battles against feelings of humiliation inspired by relations with both the mother-surrogates (sexual frustration) and the father-surrogates (professional failure) in Freud's unconscious fantasy life.

The two best recent reinterpretations in English of the Irma dream—Elms's and Erikson's—have respectively emphasized the feminine and the masculine side of its fantasies. Elms argues that the sixth pregnancy of Freud's wife, Martha, at the time of the dream raised three serious issues. Her health was suffering and he was in part responsible; he wanted more attention than she could spare from her five children; he sought a form of sexual gratification that would not produce more children—the sixth had been unplanned. Otto was the Freud family physician; probably he had examined Martha (as he examined Irma in the dream) during his visit. Martha's imminent birthday party has a double meaning—it also refers to the birth of a child. Irma is associated with pregnancy and thus with Martha not only by the pains in her abdomen in the dream, but also by her real name, which probably was Anna, the name the Freuds planned to give (and did give) to their next child if it were a girl. The two years during which Freud had given injections (= insertion of penis and ejaculation) to the old lady without infection (= pregnancy) correspond to the time elapsed since the birth of the Freud's most recent child (the others having come a year apart). The kettle in the joke suggests a uterus (borrowing = sexual penetration; damaging = impregnating). The navel that is a dream's contact with the unknown suggests an umbilical cord. Dysentery with its bloody stools may symbolize a miscarriage (unconsciously desired). The unwelcome confirmation of Martha's pregnancy given by Otto after one of his examinations of her may be represented by the bad-smelling liqueur Otto gave the Freuds and that they wanted to get rid of. The flavor, *ananas* (pineapple), may stand for Anna, the unwanted fetus. Freud may have harbored a death wish against the fetus and reproached himself for it.

As for the sexual component of Freud's marriage relationship, Elms observes, condoms in those days were unreliable and interfered seriously with sexual sensation. (As another critic suggests, they were preserved in a chemical solution that smelled like some of those mentioned in the dream.)[4] Freud felt that coitus interruptus had bad psychological effects on both partners, and that masturbation was debilitating. Other contraceptive devices had not yet been perfected. Elms thinks Freud probably proposed oral sex to Martha, who refused; she was "bashful." Like Irma, Martha would not "open her mouth properly" to admit a penis (and the "white patches" in Irma's throat suggest sperm). So Freud could not help wishing for a young widow (two of these are mentioned in the dream) who would be more receptive as a sexual partner. Elms, however, seems unaware of Freud's strong condemnation of nongenital forms of sexuality: "Ethically they are reprehensible, for they degrade the love-relationship of two human beings from being a serious matter to an otiose diversion, attended neither by risk nor by spiritual participation."[5] This may be sour grapes on Freud's part, but Elms would have to prove it.

In real life Freud's sexual relations with Martha virtually ceased by 1897, probably because of the fear of pregnancy. Other dreams of the late 1890s suggest sexual frustration. Elms speculates that this situation may have led to Freud's emphasis on libido rather than memory (or anxiety) as the central causative factor of neuroses, and to his emphasis on the Oedipus complex—shifting blame for jealousy from the parent (in the event, Freud himself) entirely to the child (Freud's children) when both compete for the attention of the parent of the opposite sex. In sum, Elms adduces much circumstantial evidence to suggest rather convincingly that Freud was preoccupied with pregnancy when he had the Irma dream.[6] Whether or not this preoccupation—or sexual frustration, or both—was the core of the dream, however, only Freud himself could tell us.

The flip side of the infantile scopophilia suggested by the dream is exhibitionism, which, as Erik Erikson points out in his outstanding interpretation of the Irma dream, has been sublimated in and through Freud's adult professional life. In writing *The Interpretation of Dreams* Freud is revealing much about himself, albeit cautiously. He simultaneously employs this self-disclosure to display his prowess as an analyst. Exhibitionism implies rivalry. The key childhood memory that Freud proposes as the origin of his ambitiousness comes from when he was seven or eight. Rather than using his own chamber pot (flush toilets were not commonplace in 1863) he urinated into his parents' pot in front of them. He wanted to show his penis—and his "production"—to his parents. Middle-class children were cared for by servants and had much less physical contact with their parents than they do today. Freud's father reprimanded him, ending his scolding by saying, "The boy will come to nothing." "References to this scene are still constantly recurring in my dreams," Freud adds, "and are always linked with an enumeration of my achievements and successes, as though I wanted to say: 'You see, I *have* come to something!'" (250).

As Erikson points out, Freud had gone to bed the night before with grave doubts about whether he really could cure hysteria as he had claimed. In the Irma dream, memories of all his medical failures came to taunt him. But the dream then saved the situation by placing Otto, not Freud, in the shamed child's role of the careless, dirty "little squirt" (who had used an unsterilized hypodermic needle). Dr. M. is not spared, either. He is described as *bartlos,* which would better be translated "beardless" (i.e., with something missing) rather than "cleanshaven" as in our text. Since a prominent beard or mustache was a male badge of distinction in the Vienna of those days, Freud's choice of adjective here suggests a vengeful castrating impulse directed against this doctor. More broadly, as Freud is about to undertake his pioneering self-analysis, the Irma dream may indicate that he is struggling with "guilt over the wish to be the one-and-only who would overcome the derisive fathers [the medical establishment, and also anti-Semites in general] and unveil the mystery [of the dream as prototypical mother in whose womb we are cradled during each night's blissful oblivion]."[7]

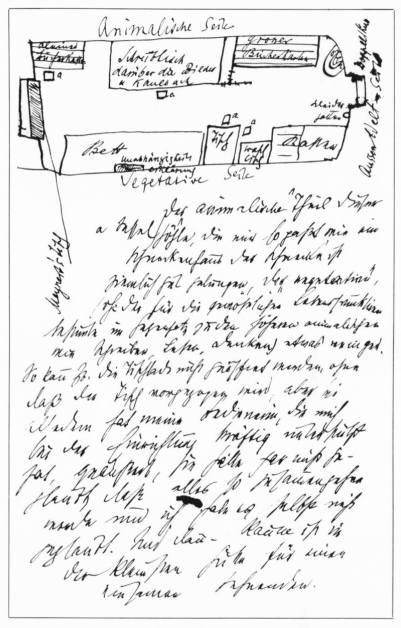

Letter from Freud to Martha Bernays, with a sketch of his quarters in the hospital, 5 October 1883. *Courtesy of the Manuscripts Division, The Library of Congress, and of Sigmund Freud Copyrights, Colchester, England.*

10

Dreams in Psychotherapy

Freud's primary rule for dream recording and for dream reporting is to write down or say the first words that occur to one in remembering a dream, no matter how absurd they may seem (493 n. 1). The analytic session during which the dream is reported is designed to resemble the circumstances of sleep. The analysand reclines on a couch at regularly appointed hours; there is no need to respond to the tranquil surroundings; the analyst sits out of view behind the analysand to eliminate visual distractions. Free association by the analysand favors hypermnesia—access to the store of memories that ordinarily remain unavailable to the waking consciousness—owing to the absence of any specified, limiting mental tasks.[1]

Freud's "Remarks on the Theory and Practice of Dream-Interpretation"[2] spell out four possible procedures for beginning a dream analysis: (1) elicit associations to the elements of the dream in the order in which they occurred as the dream was being told; (2) start with the clearest or most striking part of the dream, or with spoken words in the dream that may lead to a recollection from waking life; (3) disregard the manifest content, asking the dreamer for associations with the previous day and with the dream as a whole in general; (4)

allow the dreamer to offer any associations he or she chooses. Freud believes that the first, earliest, classical method works best for one's own dreams, but otherwise he is not sure which technique is preferable. If the second method is used, the psychoanalytic maxim "greatest distortion, strongest affect" will be useful. It is the most fantastic, bizarre, unreal detail of the dream to which the dreamer's most powerful emotions during dreaming will be related.

Resistance to recognizing the latent dream thoughts calls forth many defenses. The best defense is forgetting. The analysand may say that so much of the dream has disappeared that there is not enough left to interpret. Freud counters that the most insignificant fragments of the dream are of great importance and can lead to central meanings. Since mental events are all determined, any fragment of a dream is associatively linked with and therefore traceable to the material that has been forgotten, modified, or replaced (550–53). Psychoanalysis can often reconstruct—not the original dream itself, a matter of small importance—but all the dream thoughts from a single remaining fragment (556). Likewise, Freud regularly had patients interpret dreams they remembered from long ago exactly as if they had dreamed them the night before. When you recall something (like a dream) in the present, you show that for you it is connected to some meaning applicable to the present (560).

A defense more transparent than forgetting is for the patient to say that a certain dream need not be examined because it is unimportant or absurd. Freud answers that the judgments you make of a dream after awakening from it, and your accompanying feelings, form part of the dream's latent content and like the rest of it are subject to interpretation (482). An attempt to dismiss a dream is a clue to especially strong resistance and psychic conflicts concealed by it. Within the dream itself, absurdity points to mockery and contradiction in the dream thoughts, which may themselves attempt to neutralize threatening ideas. Absurdity in a dream may also reflect the judgment that the dreamer was foolish to do the thing she is dreaming about.[3]

Doubt about whether some detail really appeared in the dream is a secondary defense that reinforces the initial distortions and substitutions of the dream-work, and reinforces the defensive withdrawal of cathexis that has made the most critical parts of the dream often the most faint and indistinct to begin with (516). So Freud insists that the faintest possibility that something may have occurred in a dream shall be treated as equivalent to a complete certainty (555). Similarly, a dream to which the patient reacts with the self-admonition that "I must tell it to the analyst" usually conceals by reaction-formation (replacing a feeling with its exaggerated contrary) an intent to forget it. Freud gives the example of such a dream that contained a clear allusion to an affair the patient had begun during the course of analysis, and which he had resolved to conceal from the therapist (483).

Gaps and discontinuities in the dream narrative are sure signs of repression, of changing the subject before it becomes too uncomfortable; but a smoothly coherent dream report is equally suspect as the product of extensive secondary revision (528). In a sense, such dreams have already been interpreted, but in a way that avoids any embarrassment to the dreamer. To rely on a dream's specious continuity as somehow reflecting its true meaning is a sure way of misunderstanding it.[4]

The analyst does have several ways of circumventing the defenses of discontinuity and of specious unity in the dream report. Dreams often form a series continuing for weeks or even months as the dreamer grapples with the same inner conflict. Then one dream can be further interpreted with the aid of another in the same series, particularly the one immediately following it—and this is all the more true when the next dream occurs on the same night, for the contents of all dreams from the same night are closely related (563 and 369). Dreams tend to express wishes more boldly and clearly as the night wears on. Freud gives examples from a series of his own dreams expressing a longing to visit Rome (226–31), and from two dreams by a patient on the same night. The second of these helped clarify the first (397–99). In the first dream the patient's mother sent the patient's little girl away by herself and the patient felt reproachful. In the second dream the patient identified herself with her brother, who was being threatened with castration by the mother. Putting the two dreams together, Freud connected the sending away of "the little one" (= the penis) with castration, and concluded that the ultimate meaning of the dreams was the dreamer's reproach to her mother for not having conceived her as a boy.

Even when only one dream is available, Freud finds that a most effective technique for exposing the weak points in its defensive disguise is to have the dreamer retell it once some time has elapsed since the first telling. Being asked to repeat a dream warns the dreamer that special attention will be paid to it; so he or she instinctively hastens to shore up the weak points in the defenses of the dream by replacing the more revealing expressions by others. The details modified during the retelling will prove the most stressful and significant (553–54). This theory, however, has not been supported by empirical research, although the final verdict is not yet in.[5]

The most reliable direct clues to a dream's true meanings are its accompanying affects (feelings), because these are the portions of the latent content that undergo the least distortion as they pass over into the manifest content (106 and 497–98). Of course these feelings usually become weakened during sleep, when the quiescence of the body tends to dull all impressions. A partial canceling-out of feelings also occurs since they, like other mental events, are all linked to their contradictory opposite in the unconscious. And above all, after the censorship has distorted and disguised the dream, its next task is to inhibit the feelings associated with it so that they will be less disturbing to the dreamer and not provoke awakening (505–6). At the opposite extreme, a feeling that seems inappropriately strong for the situation in a dream is a clue that repression has been released: you are now allowing yourself to feel something that you previously thought you should not feel.

Of course displacement can redirect a dream feeling from its real object to another one. And a feeling in the latent content may be replaced by its contrary in the manifest content in accordance with Freud's rule of interpretation, which states that any part of a dream can represent its opposite as readily as itself (508 and 353). Freud thinks that the most common transformation of affects in a dream is from repressed sexual excitement to overt anxiety. But only the context of the dreamer's situation and associations can decide which affect is replacing which other. Wish fulfillment may replace a disagreeable feeling with its opposite; similarly, waking life often requires us to conceal our hostility and to act friendly toward someone we dislike (509). For example, one day an elderly man suffering from a serious disease had a crisis that forced him to face the possibility of dying. Shortly before the crisis, he had failed to get an erection to have intercourse with his sympathetic wife. He woke up laughing uproariously after a dream where "I was lying in bed and a gentleman who was known to me entered the room; I tried to turn on the light but was unable to; I tried over and over again, but in vain. Thereupon my wife got out of bed to help me, but she could not manage it either." The familiar gentleman was Death, "the great Unknown" (a phrase that had gone through the dreamer's mind the previous day; the dream changed it into its opposite). The old man felt like weeping at the realization that he was physically deteriorating, had become impotent, and soon must die; the dream-work managed to transform these gloomy thoughts into a comic scene. But even there the light (= life) could not be lit, and the dreamer was deeply depressed (the authentic affect) the next day (510).

To illustrate the interpretation of affects in dreams, Freud presents his "*non vixit*" dream.

> I had gone to Brücke's laboratory at night, and, in response to a gentle knock on the door, I opened it to [the late] Professor Fleischl, who came in with a number of strangers and, after exchanging a few words, sat down at the table. [Dream #2] My friend Fliess had come to Vienna unobtrusively in July. I met him on the street in conversation with my [deceased] friend P., and went with them to some place where they sat opposite each other as though they were at a small table. I sat in front at its narrow end. Fliess spoke about his sister and said that in three quarters of an hour she was dead, and added some such words as "that was the threshold." As P. failed to understand him, Fliess turned to me and asked me how much I had told P. about his affairs. Whereupon, overcome by strange

emotions, I tried to explain to Fliess that P. (could not understand anything at all, of course, because he) was not alive. But what I actually said—and I myself noticed the mistake—was "NON VIXIT" [in Latin, "He did not live" instead of *Non vivit*, "he was not alive"]. I then gave P. a piercing look. Under my gaze he turned pale; his form grew indistinct and his eyes a sickly blue—and finally he melted away. I was highly delighted at this and I now realized that Ernst Fleischl, too, had been no more than an apparition, a [ghost]; and it seemed to me quite possible that people of that kind only existed as long as one liked and could be got rid of if someone else wanted it (456–57).

Freud's initial associations are that the key episode of the dream—annihilating P. with a glance—constitutes a wish-fulfilling reversal of a moment when Freud felt annihilated by a glare from Brücke's striking blue eyes when he came in late for his job as a demonstrator in the old man's physiological laboratory. P. was being punished by Freud in the dream because after he replaced Freud in that laboratory job, he knew he had not long to live and was impatient for a promotion. Since Fleischl, one of Brücke's two assistants (the position that P. coveted) was also quite ill, P.'s open wish to have him out of the way could be interpreted as a wish for Fleischl's death—and Fleischl was a friend of Freud's.

At the same time Freud felt affection for this former coworker P., and admired his talents as a scientist. So in the dream he memorialized him. (Only a few days before the dream, which occurred on 16 October 1898, Freud had attended a university ceremony on the occasion of the unveiling of a monument to the late Fleischl.) Freud traced the Latin *non vixit* to his memory of an inscription on a monument to a former kaiser of Austria: "Saluti patriae vixit / Non diu sed totus." (He lived for the good of his fatherland, not long, but completely.) (The actual inscription read *publicae* [for the public] rather than *patriae*; Freud's unconscious substitution reflects a latent identification of his and P.'s mutual superior, Brücke, with a father-figure.) A further association of Freud's traces his mixed feelings of admiration and anger toward P. to a speech by Brutus in Shakespeare's *Julius*

Caesar (act 3, scene 2): "As Caesar loved me, I weep for him; as he was fortunate, I rejoice at it; as he was valiant, I honour him; but, as he was ambitious, I slew him." Freud now realizes that he has been playing the part of Brutus in the dream. Since Fliess never actually visited Vienna in *July* (the month named after *Julius* Caesar), the inaccurate detail that he had done so confirms the identification with Brutus in Freud's mind. Freud now recalls having actually played Brutus in a scene with Caesar taken from a play by Schiller. *Kaiser* (on the monument; see above) is a variant form of the word *Caesar*. So the monument to the first is associated with honoring the second as well. Freud's nephew John, a year older than he and who had played Caesar in that same scene, is associated with P. in Freud's mind as a superior rival. The phrase "*non vixit*" is overdetermined by memories of a childhood scene: Freud's father scolded him for hitting John; Freud protested that John had hit him first. The third-person singular form of *wichsen*, the child's verb for "hit" in German, sounds like the Latin *vixit*. So ultimately Freud's ambivalent feelings toward P. in the dream come from an unconscious identification of P. with John (460).

One can speculate that Freud also desired promotion in the physiological lab. It would have been possible only if his sick friend died. So Freud could not admit this desire to himself, much as he hoped to remain in academic life as a researcher. Therefore it was all the more intolerable to hear that desire expressed openly by someone else because that person was allowing himself liberties that Freud's own conscience would not allow him to take: he was doubly jealous.

Later in *The Interpretation of Dreams*, Freud describes the day residue of the "*non vixit*" dream. His friend Fliess in Berlin had just undergone an operation; the preliminary results were worrisome. Fliess's sister had died young after a brief illness; Freud was concerned lest his friend's constitution prove equally delicate. Freud wished to visit Fliess immediately but had not done so because of a large boil on his perineum that made any movement painful. Consciously, he felt ashamed of not going. He feared he would hear that Fliess was worsening, or that he would make the trip to see him after all, only to arrive too late. He would then reproach himself strongly. Through an association to impressions with a similar feeling tone, in the dream Freud represented his present feelings of shame with memories of the humiliating moment when he had been reprimanded for being remiss in his duties by coming late to Brücke's lab many years before (518–19). With hindsight, we can suspect that the detail of Fliess's imaginary journey to Vienna in July identifies Fliess as well as John and P. with Caesar; so Freud's anxiety about Fliess's operation conceals a repressed death wish against his friend, from whom, within two years, he would indeed be estranged. On the surface, Fliess's imaginary journey represents a wish-fulfilling reversal of the real situation ("I can't go see him, but he can come see me").

Freud's anger in the dream covers an uneasy feeling that he might be betraying Fliess. This had been reinforced shortly before the dream. Fliess's relatives passed on news of how Freud's friend was doing after his operation, but asked Freud to tell no one else about it. In this request Freud felt a veiled suspicion that he might be indiscreet. It stung because in the past Freud had indeed been indiscreet; he had repeated one friend's unfavorable comments to another friend who was their object. And one of these two friends was Fleischl. He defends himself against the charge of indiscretion by turning P. into a ghost (you cannot tell secrets to a dead person). In this way, although he does not own it, Freud is also getting back at Fleischl for having reproached him in the past. Freud's present anger over the implied charge of indiscretion is reinforced by memories of "hostile feelings against persons of whom [he] was in reality fond" (520). He adds that in a sense all his friends have been reincarnations (ghosts, as it were) of his beloved first enemy, his childhood playmate John. In one of the most revealing passages of *The Interpretation of Dreams,* Freud concludes, "My emotional life has always insisted that I should have an intimate friend and a hated enemy. I have always been able to provide myself afresh with both, and it has not infrequently happened that the ideal situation of childhood has been so completely reproduced that friend and enemy have come together in a single individual" (521). As Freud's analysis of the "*non vixit*" dream shows, exploring the feelings in a dream can not only uncover entire constellations of memories, but also reveal the dreamer's whole emotional life-style, established early in childhood.

As a therapist, Freud naturally wondered whether phenomena related to dreams—daydreams and the delusions of madness—could be equally helpful in the course of an analysis. Freud believed that we experience many preconscious fantasies (confusingly, Freud uses the term *unconscious* to mean *preconscious* when discussing daydreams) as well as conscious ones both during our waking hours and during sleep. He found that such fantasies frequently appeared as the forerunners of hysterical symptoms. Unlike dreams, they are not hallucinatory—not perceived as real. Like dreams, he said, they fulfill wishes, derive from infantile experiences, and emerge when the censorship has relaxed. They may be taken over to provide prefabricated portions of dreams; during sleep they can sometimes emerge to consciousness, where they form relatively coherent units of the dream narrative in contrast with the most incoherent surrounding material (529–31).[6]

The relationship between dreams and madness remains an open question. Freud hoped to have his investigation of dreams contribute to an understanding of mental disorders (658), but instead he found himself extrapolating from his knowledge of neurosis and madness in order to explain dreams. In his review of his precursors' work (119–24) Freud cites many case studies that show how a mental disorder first makes its appearance in the dream life, and how traces of it persist there after the patient has apparently been cured. Freud is convinced that the key to a psychological understanding of dreams and delusions is that both are wish fulfillments. As Freud well knew, however, dreams are not in themselves pathological: all healthy people dream.[7] Psychosis occurs when unconscious impulses overwhelm the censorship of the waking self, flood the preconscious, and thus gain control over our words and deeds, or when they take over our organs of sense perception and cause hallucinatory regression (607). But Freud observed cases where a person suffering from delusions might have normal-appearing dreams and vice versa.[8] Dreams are not a surefire index of mental health.

Freud, however, did not work with psychotics. A recent empirical comparison of the dreams of thirty schizophrenics with the same number of nonpsychotic persons showed unequivocal differences between the dreams of the two groups. Schizophrenics' dreams characteristically depicted a stressful situation or an emergency. The people and the setting in such dreams were "overwhelmingly threatening." The dreamers were trapped or lost; unlike normal subjects, they found no escape by the end of the dream. Bloody dismemberment and brutal mutilation were common, as was a feeling of loss of control over mental functioning. In contrast, the normal dreams were filled with a variety of coping techniques (not always successful); they tended to be relatively quite realistic, practical, and efficient. The study concludes that bizarre primary process thinking "may be in large part a function of the degree of maladjustment of the dreamer, and not necessarily a sine qua non of dream life. . . . The greater the resources of the awake ego, the more successfully will the dream deal with emotional conflicts, and achieve ego reintegration during sleep."[9] One can observe a similar phenomenon in children's dreams, which become less "trapped" and hopeless as their ego functioning matures.

11

Conclusion:
Challenges to Freud

From the standpoint of Freudian orthodoxy, in recent decades on the American scene the use of dreams in psychotherapy has fallen on hard times. The most militant Freudians do not talk much about dreams. Those who interpret them most enthusiastically are the heretical Jungians and some "third force" psychologists. Both these schools find inhibition and impulse less important than an instinctual "third force": the drive toward realizing one's full potential through what is variously called "ego-synthesis," "self-actualization," or "self-realization." Such analysts see dreams essentially as coded messages from a wise unconscious that strives to make itself understood so that it can benefit the conscious self.[1] Such an approach rejects the characteristically Freudian insistence on the repressed past to focus on the dreamer's current situation and problems. And the tragic sense of life's limitations is sacrificed to an optimism that Freud deplored as the symptom of a shallow, materialistic society.

In France the "return to Freud" led by the late Jacques Lacan proved enormously influential in the sixties and seventies. The movement sought to recuperate Freud's original, revolutionary meanings—particularly regarding psychic repression—that had been sugarcoated by his followers. But this group's philosophical training and resulting love of abstractions diverted it from publishing detailed case histories or reporting dreams. A few of Freud's dreams are sometimes discussed, but in a fragmentary way subordinated to nondream topics.[2] Centered in England, the object-relations school of psychoanalysis (Balint, Fairbairn, Guntrip, Klein, Kohut, Mahler, Winnicott) has richly developed Freudian theory by stressing that the origins of mental disorders lie in the pre-Oedipal period when mother-child relationships and the establishment of trust are essential (rather than in Oedipal rivalry). This school still uses dreams to provide insight, but they no longer are privileged over other sources of information. Calvin Hall in the United States has led the dream researchers who remain true to Freudian theory while attempting to support it with extensive theoretical dream research and statistical compilations under rigorous experimental conditions.

In recent years Freud's basic understanding of what a dream is has come under attack. In chapter 4 we pointed out that sleep research suggests that Freud's theories apply only to ordinary vividly remembered dreams, and not to NREM musings, nightmares, night terrors, and posttraumatic anxiety dreams. A more radical critique was the "activation-synthesis" hypothesis, published in 1977, which proposed that dreams arise not from unconscious impulses, but from physiologically determined nerve-cell activity in the primitive brain stem during sleep. Dreams occur when the highly evolved forebrain tries to make sense of these chaotic neural impulses. This hypothesis, however, was exploded the following year.[3]

The most serious and sustained challenge to Freudian dream theory has come from David Foulkes, who has been strongly influenced by the developmental psychology of Jean Piaget. His research strongly suggests that dreaming is a cognitive skill akin to and dependent upon the ability to verbalize. It lags behind the child's waking ability to verbalize, and matures fully only sometime after the seventh year of life—perhaps even after the onset of puberty. He sharply criticizes Freud's notion that an unconscious wish is the primary, indispensable instigator of dreams; he says that during dreaming our minds are organized in a recollective rather than an encoding mode. Dreaming, Foulkes sums up, is a symbolic act that develops together with our capacity to symbolize: this capacity is learned, not built into the unconscious.[4] His arguments are highly plausible regarding the nature of children's dreams in and of themselves. But he does not eliminate the possibility that what children experience while dreaming may be different from what they can report in words, for children's powerful, inarticulate emotions are indisputably present after the first few months of life. He does nothing to explain the overdetermination and distortions of adult dreams. And he certainly does not disprove that adult dreams may retrospectively enact childhood feelings. What he does establish is that art and play therapy rather than dream analysis are the treatments of choice for preschool children. We should remember that Freud himself neither psychoanalyzed children nor claimed that dream interpretation would let us do so.

Feminist critics have launched a more fundamental attack. If the basis of Freud's theories is sexuality, and if he does not understand women, how can his psychology be worth anything at all? Some feel that his famous question to Marie Bonaparte, "What does a woman want?" reveals a shocking lack of insight in an analyst many of whose patients were women. And his aphorism "anatomy is destiny" offensively reaffirms the status quo that oppresses women by relegating them to the role of childbearers and caretakers. Even Freud's sympathetic biographer Ernest Jones said Freud thought women's main function was "to be ministering angels to the needs and comforts of men" (2:421). In *The Interpretation of Dreams* these attitudes are less in evidence, and consequently less of an interference, than elsewhere. In this book the most obvious blindness to women appears in the lack of breast (from a woman's viewpoint) and clitoris symbolism—and, more subtly, in the quiet absence of a specifically female point of view in general. Freud was not sexually experienced. He firmly believed that the only good female orgasm was vaginal. So any desire for clitoral stimulation would be a vestige of a sexually immature, childish, masturbatory orientation—in a word, neurotic. He did not seem to realize that stimulation of either clitoris or vagina may produce an orgasm centered either in the stimulated organ, or in the other, or in both. His assumption that the insertion of a penis provides the only legitimate form of female sexual gratification defies anatomical realities.

Two even more objectionable Freudian notions are not prominent in *The Interpretation of Dreams*: the idea that women suffer from "penis envy," a deep-seated sense of bodily inferiority to men; and that men achieve a superior, more rigorous superego (moral) development. The latter implies that women are more emotional, less just, and less altruistic or adaptable.[5] As for the first idea, Freud did once suggest that penis envy is found only in some neurotic women; he said that others have replaced the child's wish for a penis by the wish for a baby—although, he added, these two wishes are "fundamentally identical." And toward the end of his life, in both "The Question of Lay Analysis" (1926) and again in "Analysis Terminable and Interminable" (1937) he regressed to stating flatly that penis envy was universal in women.[6] If we recognize the penis as symbolizing the unfair advantages often granted men by society (Freud, of course, never said any such thing), envy in some women seems more plausible.

At least Freud was not a rigid sexist insofar as he recognized a fundamental bisexuality in all human beings: in 1901 he wrote that he had encountered "a very considerable current of [latent] homosexuality" in every analysis of either sex that he had conducted.[7] He was attracted to strong, intellectual women like Lou Andreas-Salomé and Marie Bonaparte as friends. And his own youngest daughter Anna became a prominent psychoanalyst with his support. As for his opinion on women's moral development, the reader might reflect on whether it is men or women who are mainly starving, torturing, and killing innocent people in the real world, and thus dismiss Freud's statement. Or, in fairness to him, consider the passage immediately following the one concerning the relationship between gender and moral development: "pure masculinity and femininity remain theoretical constructions of uncertain content"; all human beings combine traits from both "sexes" (*SE* 19:258).

Freud's dream theory becomes entangled in his questionable sex-typing views in the "Dora" case history. When Freud had completed

Conclusion: Challenges to Freud

The Interpretation of Dreams, he realized he had provided no complete, detailed example of dream interpretation in the context of an analysis to support his theories. So the next year (although it was not published until 1905) he wrote up the "Fragment of an Analysis of a Case of Hysteria," which prominently features two of the patient's dreams. "Dora" was a teenager who had become close friends with a couple, Herr and Frau K. Her father was having an affair with Frau K. Frustrated, Herr K. seduced and abandoned the K. governess, who was then disowned by her own family. Dora learned of this. Then Herr K. grabbed and kissed Dora when she was fourteen. She felt disgusted and pushed him away, but he remained attentive to her, and propositioned her when she was sixteen. She complained to her mother. The three other adults betrayed her. Frau K. said Dora was obsessed with sex (which Frau K. had encouraged Dora to discuss with her); Herr K. denied everything; and Dora's father took her to Freud against her will, to cure her of her "delusions." Dora then understood that she had been used as a pawn in a sexual exchange: the tacit agreement was that Herr K. could try to seduce her undisturbed so long as he did not interfere with Frau K.'s affair with Dora's father.

Freud betrayed her in turn. He found her distaste for marriage and motherhood unreasonable; he did not take seriously her preference for an intellectual life, and was very directive in the therapy: he told Dora she was secretly in love with Herr K., that she had a fantasy of performing fellatio on him, and that she should agree to marry Herr K.—whom Freud found not unattractive. He believed her story of Herr K.'s pursuit of her, but refused to support her in making the guilty adults confess what had really happened. Not only her shaky adolescent sense of identity but also her very perception of reality was being attacked on all sides. Even if Dora did feel attraction to Herr K., she clearly was not ready for marriage, and she knew she had no more guarantees of his loyalty than the governess (on whom he had used the same line) had had. She broke off the analysis.

For years, Freud's ingenious interpretations of Dora's dreams and his masterful literary presentation of the case masked the fact (which he himself owned frankly) that he had mishandled it badly. Given the nature of society, the medical profession, and psychological understanding in 1901, Freud probably did as well as anyone else could have done.[8] It seems likely that Freud, frustrated in what had become a sexless marriage, unconsciously identified himself with Herr K. and hoped to pair him with his desired object, Dora, as a way of gaining vicarious satisfaction for himself. To do so, he had to imagine Dora as a mature woman, ready to respond to passion with passion, rather than as a troubled adolescent undergoing what Erik Erikson was later to call an "identity crisis." In Dora's unending series of psychosomatic ailments Freud accurately recognized a devious, manipulative way of defying male authority and evading her manifest destiny of housework and child-rearing. Dora's strategy for secret rebellion worked badly. She made herself and everyone else miserable. But the accepted psychiatric procedure at the time was to crush such resistance in female patients rather than trying to direct it into paths more constructive than illness.[9]

Freud learned from the experience and the entire psychoanalytic movement benefited. He later admitted that Dora had suffered from his excessive concern for proving his theories rather than helping her, and that he had been unaware of her identification of him with her father. And nine years later Freud began to speak of the countertransference, of the analyst's projecting her or his own fantasies onto the patient. The negative assessment of Freud's therapeutic failure above may tempt us to forget that it led to numerous fruitful developments in his subsequent theory and practice—from which all later psychotherapists have profited, as have their patients.

The Dora case does raise the issue of how well Freud knew himself. The father of psychoanalysis never was psychoanalyzed, except by himself. So how solid is the basis of the discipline he created? The person with whom Freud probably came closest to an analysand's role was Carl Jung. The two men exchanged dreams and interpreted each other's. But when Jung asked for the intimate details of Freud's sexual and childhood feelings necessary to complete the interpretations, he was shocked to find that Freud refused to divulge these because "I cannot risk my authority" as leader of the psychoanalytic movement.[10]

Conclusion: Challenges to Freud

Undoubtedly Freud could have learned more and missed less by being analyzed. But he spent half an hour a day in self-examination; he owned enough (nonsexual) disagreeable impulses in *The Interpretation of Dreams* to demonstrate convincingly his modesty and honesty; and had he publicly confessed his sexual feelings he would have risked being labeled a degenerate and dismissed as a madman by critics who forget we are not responsible for our fantasies, and that thoughts and actions are two different things.[11] How thoroughly Freud knew himself in private, we shall never know.

A conscientious recent overview of the tested validity of Freud's ideas examined hundreds of empirical case studies and took into account all those whose design seemed scientifically defensible. There seems to be partial support for the idea that at least one of the functions of dreams is to provide a safety valve to relieve psychic stress. Not supported are the notions that dreams are disguised fulfillments of unconscious wishes, nor that they function as the "guardians of sleep" (according to the technical criterion of brain-wave measurements, we briefly wake during half of our REM periods).[12]

After almost a century it is not surprising that elements of Freud's dream theories have been disproven. Compared to other hypotheses in the history of science, Freud's have been quite durable. "All theories are evanescent . . . their potency lies primarily in the new vistas for research and thought that they provide. In these terms, Freud's models have already proven themselves spectacularly."[13] Freud ranks with Aristotle, Galileo, and Newton as a pioneering scientific thinker whose work has lasting timeliness and vitality. The concept of a dynamic unconscious has affected every corner of our intellectual life. Freud has created such a wide-ranging, fecund frame of reference that even his severest critics often think in his terms as they attack him. The notions of mental defenses and symbolic behavior, so richly illustrated in *The Interpretation of Dreams,* have pervaded our awareness to the point of becoming second nature.

Notes

1. Historical Context

1. Henri F. Ellenberger, *The Discovery of the Unconscious: The History and Evolution of Dynamic Psychology* (New York: Basic Books, 1970), 453–54. Further references are indicated parenthetically in the text.

2. Ernest Jones, *The Life and Work of Sigmund Freud*, 3 vols. (New York: Basic Books, 1953–57), 1:235–42. Further references are indicated parenthetically in the text.

3. Ellenberger, *Discovery*, 539–40, n. 497. For a full comparison of the ideas of these two great psychologists, see Henri-Jean Barraud, *Freud et Janet: Étude comparée* (Toulouse: Édouard Privet, 1971).

4. With this concept Janet anticipated the post-Freudian development of "ego psychology," which was first clearly defined in a book by Heinz Hartmann the year that Freud died. Once again, Janet failed to get credit.

2. The Importance of the Work

1. See Laurence M. Porter, *The Literary Dream in French Romanticism: A Psychoanalytical Interpretation* (Detroit: Wayne State University Press, 1979), xi–xiv and 13–23, for background on the prehistory of depth psychology in the century before Freud.

2. See Erik H. Erikson's masterful demonstrations of this thesis in *Childhood and Society, Young Man Luther*, and *Gandhi's Truth*.

3. The founder of social work was "Anna O." (Berthe Pappenheim), who started out as a hysterical patient of Freud's erstwhile mentor and collaborator, Josef Breuer.

3. Critical Reception

1. Sigmund Freud, *The Interpretation of Dreams*, ed. and trans. James Strachey (New York: Avon Books, 1980 [1965]), xxiv. Future references to this edition will be indicated by page numbers alone, in parentheses in the text.

2. For full references to the other critics mentioned see the Select Bibliography.

3. For a rollicking exposé of the fringes of Freudian criticism, see Janet Malcolm, *In the Freud Archives* (New York: Knopf, 1984).

4. See also I. Bry and A. H. Rifkin, "Freud and the History of Ideas: Primary Sources, 1886–1910," *Science and Psychoanalysis* 5 (1962):20–23.

5. See Bry and Rifkin, "Freud and the History of Ideas," 24–29, and Hannah S. Decker, *Freud in Germany: Revolution and Reaction in Science, 1893–1907* Psychological Issues, no. 41. (New York: International Universities Press, 1977), 262–69 and 276–92. Further references to Decker follow parenthetically in the text.

6. See Carl Gustav Jung, "Sigmund Freud," in *Memories, Dreams, Reflections*, recorded and edited by Aniela Jaffé, trans. Richard and Clara Winston (New York: Random House, 1961), 146–69. See also Carl Gustav Jung, *Collected Works*, ed. Herbert Read, Michael Fordman, and Gerhard Adler, 17 vols. (New York: Pantheon Books, 1953–73), vol. 4, *Freud and Psychoanalysis*, and Jung's two essays on Freud in *Collected Works*, vol. 15, *The Spirit in Man, Art, and Literature*, 33–49.

7. Carl Gustav Jung, "In Memory of Sigmund Freud," in *Collected Works*, 15:44.

8. Jung, *Memories, Dreams, Reflections*, 168–69.

4. Introduction: Defining Sleep and Dreams

1. See J. A. Horne, "Mammalian Sleep Function in Particular Reference to Man," in *Sleep Mechanisms and Functions in Humans and Animals: An Evolutionary Perspective*, ed. Andrew Richard Mayes (Wokingham, Berkshire, England: Van Nostrand Reinhold, 1983), 288–89.

2. In hibernation, a much stronger, more prolonged stimulus is needed to arouse animals than during sleep. In hibernation and torpor (in nonmammals), season or temperature rather than the twenty-four-hour cycle is associated with the state. In coma, no stimulus elicits a response. For these definitions I am indebted to Harold Zepelin.

Cats, dogs, foxes, hedgehogs, and cattle frequently enter a state of drowsiness. They seem relaxed, look sleepy, and show a distinctive brain-wave pattern different from that of waking, but they respond to stimuli much less intense than those needed to arouse them from sleep (Ray Meddis, "The Evolution of Sleep," in *Sleep Mechanisms*, ed. Mayes, 59).

3. One of the most promising candidates for the role of a natural sleep substance is glycopeptide, which has been isolated from human urine. It has been shown to induce a 50 percent increase in slow-wave sleep in animals. This substance may be derived from bacterial waste products absorbed through the walls of the intestines. See Thomas H. Maugh II, "Sleep-Promoting Factor Isolated," *Science*, 25 June 1982. The first comprehensive overview of the entire question has just appeared in *Endogenous Sleep Substances and Sleep Regulation*, ed. S. Inoué and A. A. Borbély (Utrecht, the Netherlands: VNU Science Press, 1985) (publications of the Taniguchi Symposia on Brain Sciences, no. 8, held in Japan, 1984).

4. See Truett Allison and Henry Van Twyver, "The Sleep and Dreams of Animals," in *The New World of Dreams*, ed. Ralph L. Woods and Herbert B. Greenhouse (New York: Macmillan, 1974), 344–45.

5. See Harold Zepelin and A. Rechtschaffen, "Mammalian Sleep, Longevity, and Energy Metabolism," *Brain, Behavior, and Evolution* 10 (1974):425–76; Zepelin, "A Life Span Perspective on Sleep," in *Sleep Mechanisms*, ed. Mayes, 126; and Ray Meddis, "The Evolution of Sleep," in *Sleep Mechanisms*, ed. Mayes, 61–66, 69, and 71.

6. Gay Gaer Luce, "The Dream Cycle throughout the Night," in *New World*, ed. Woods and Greenhouse, 282.

7. An intense REM dream may awaken you for good, especially in the morning. For a summary of information on sleep and dream cycles see Luce, 278–86.

8. William C. Dement, *Some Must Watch While Some Must Sleep* (New York: Simon & Schuster, 1976), 28–30. Zepelin and Rechtschaffen point out that REM sleep as a percentage of total sleep time cannot be correlated with the size or intelligence of mammalian species. Newborn guinea pigs have little REM sleep; newborn hamsters, rats, puppies, and kittens have only REM sleep. Monkeys spend much less time in REM sleep than do humans, but elephants and opossums spend much more.

9. See Ismet Karacan et al., "Some Characteristics of Nocturnal Penile Tumescence in Young Adults," *Archives of General Psychiatry* 26 (April 1972):351–56; and Herbert Greenhouse, "Penile Erections during Dreams," in *New World*, ed. Woods and Greenhouse, 296–97.

10. See T. Okuma, E. Fukuyama, and K. Kobayashi, "'Dream Detector' and Comparison of Laboratory and Home Dreams Collected by REMP [REM-period] Awakening Technique," *Advances in Sleep Research* 2 (1976):229.

11. It is possible that activity in the right hemisphere of the brain produces vivid, bizarre dreams, whereas left hemisphere activity leads to verbal, rational, analytic thinking during sleep. See Alan Leboeuf, Patricia McKay,

and Keith Clarke, "Lateral Eye Movements and Dream Recall in Males: A Re-Appraisal," *Imagination, Cognition and Personality* 3, no. 1 (1983–84):62.

12. For this classification, and for details in the next four paragraphs, I am indebted to Ernest Hartmann, *The Nightmare: The Psychology and Biology of Terrifying Dreams* (New York: Basic Books, 1984). See also Hartmann, "From the Biology of Dreaming to the Biology of the Mind," *Psychoanalytic Study of the Child* 37 (1982):303–35.

13. Freud confused night terrors and nightmares. See *Interpretation of Dreams*, 624–25.

5. The Origins of Psychoanalysis

1. *Introductory Lectures on Psycho-Analysis*, in *The Standard Edition of the Complete Psychological Works of Sigmund Freud*, ed. and trans. James Strachey, 24 vols. (London: Hogarth, 1953–74), 15:144. Henceforth all references to this edition, abbreviated *SE*, will be so indicated parenthetically in the text.

2. For good clear summaries of Freud's "Project" and its sources, see Ellenberger, *Discovery*, 478–80, and Ernst Kris, Introduction to *The Origins of Psycho-Analysis: Letters to Wilhelm Fliess, Drafts and Notes, 1887–1902*, ed. Marie Bonaparte, Anna Freud, and Ernst Kris (Garden City, N.Y.: Doubleday Anchor, 1957), 14–26.

3. See "Fragment of an Analysis of a Case of Hysteria," *SE* 7:113, and Letter of 1908, in *The Freud-Jung Letters*, ed. William McGuire (Princeton University Press, 1974), 140–41. For this entire discussion I am indebted to the fine article by Barry Silverstein, "Freud's Psychology and Its Organic Foundation: Sexuality and Mind-Body Interactionism," *Psychoanalytic Review* 72, no. 2 (Summer 1985):204–28.

4. See also Thomas Nagel, "Freud's Anthropomorphism," in *Philosophers on Freud: New Evaluations*, ed. Richard Wollheim (New York: Jason Aronson, 1974), 11–24. In *The Interpretation of Dreams* Freud abandoned the ambition that he had cherished in the "Project" of locating specific nerve pathways with discrete functions in the brain, but not until 1915 did he renounce the hope that advances in the anatomical study of the nervous system would provide a detailed map of the brain; and he retained the model of an energy transmission system even after that date. On this see Robert C. Solomon, "Freud's Neurological Theory of Mind," in *Philosophers on Freud*, ed. Wollheim, 25–52.

5. Letter of 27 January 1908, in *Freud-Jung Letters*, ed. William McGuire, 115–16.

6. See "Some Thoughts on Development and Repression—Aetiology," *Introductory Lectures*, no. 22, in *SE* 16:352; and "On Psychotherapy," *SE*

Notes

7:267. "Frustration" translates the German *Versagung*, which covers both external and self-imposed denials of desire. After the *Introductory Lectures* Freud virtually abandons the frustration theory of the etiology of neurosis, and reemphasizes the pathogenic role of trauma instead.

7. "Delusions and Dreams in Jensen's *Gradiva*," *SE* 9:90.

8. "Remarks on the Theory and Practice of Dream Interpretation" (1923), *SE* 19:117.

9. "Five Lectures on Psychoanalysis" (1910), *SE* 11:33.

10. See Leonard Shengold, "The Metaphor of the Journey in *The Interpretation of Dreams*," *American Imago* 23 (1966):316–31.

11. Letter of 3 October 1897, in *The Complete Letters of Sigmund Freud to Wilhelm Fliess, 1887–1904*, ed. and trans. Jeffrey Moussaieff Masson (Cambridge, Mass.: Harvard University Press, Belknap Press, 1985), 268. For whatever unconscious reasons of his own, Masson has suppressed all reference to this crucial passage in his extensive index.

Among the numerous speculations on Freud's Oedipus complex, the best are Siegfried Bernfeld, "An Unknown Autobiographical Fragment by Freud," *American Imago* 4, no. 1 (August 1946):3–19; Kenneth A. Grigg, "'All Roads Lead to Rome': The Role of the Nursemaid in Freud's Dreams," *American Psychological Association: Journal* 21 (1973):108–26; Stanley Edgar Hyman, *The Tangled Bank: Darwin, Marx, Frazer and Freud as Imaginative Writers* (New York: Atheneum, 1962), 324–32; Ann Vannan Rankin, "The Three Generations: Freud's Hasdrubal/Hamilcar Barca Error," *American Imago* 20, no. 4 (1963):403–9; and Jim Swan, "*Mater* and Nannie: Freud's Two Mothers and the Discovery of the Oedipus Complex," *American Imago* 31, no. 1 (Spring 1974):1–64—especially the last.

12. "The Development of the Libido and the Sexual Organizations," *Introductory Lectures*, no. 21, *SE* 16:321.

13. "The Sexual Life of Human Beings," *Introductory Lectures*, no. 20, *SE* 16:313; and "The Development of the Libido," no. 21, *SE* 16:321.

14. Freud was well aware that his psychology of the ego was underdeveloped, and that he had not commented on the ego as something that could grow and develop in its own right. He left that task to later researchers, although he did explicitly describe maturation as the gradual conquest of the id's territory by the ego: "Where id was, ego shall be."

15. *SE* 11:25–27.

16. "The Libido Theory and Narcissism," *Introductory Lectures*, no. 26, *SE* 16:419.

17. Freud was an atheist. "Mystical" as used here refers to his sense of the mystery of humanness rather than to his belief in a transcendent deity. He thought that the purpose of religion was to restrain sexual impulses by providing them with a sublimated outlet in worship, and to alleviate individuals'

isolation by providing them with a larger community than the family. See "From the History of an Infantile Neurosis" (1918), *SE* 17:114–15.

18. The foregoing discussion of translations is drawn from Bruno Bettelheim's eloquent *Freud and Man's Soul* (1982; reprint ed. New York: Vintage Books, 1984), 9–10, 65–78, et passim. New translations will become possible when the German copyright to Freud's works expires at the end of the 1980s.

6. Manifest Content: The Facade of Dreams

1. See also "Wish-Fulfilment," *Introductory Lectures,* no. 14, *SE* 15:221–24.

2. Freud claims a wish always is required in order to mobilize the day residue (594–96). On the relationship of sleep to narcissism, see "A Metapsychological Supplement to the Theory of Dreams" (1917), *SE* 14:224–26.

3. Freud does not explore another fantasy that arises in connection with his dream. In it he contracts glaucoma, the eye disease from which his father suffered. He goes incognito to his friend Fliess's house in Berlin and has himself operated on. He has the secret satisfaction of knowing that the cocaine anesthetic used for the operation has been discovered by himself.

An orthodox psychoanalytic reading might claim that this fantasy combines symbolic castration with repressed passive homosexuality. If as Freud claims elsewhere, death = castration = blindness in the symbolic sphere, then Freud, unconsciously relieved and liberated by his rival father's death (only then did he begin his self-analysis and the composition of his masterpiece, *The Interpretation of Dreams*), would be punishing himself by taking his father's blindness upon himself. At the same time, the idea of having his helpless, passive body operated on in the presence of Fliess suggests an unconscious desire to have Fliess handle and manipulate his body. Years later, at any rate, Freud owned that some traces of "unruly homosexual feeling" had been present in him during their relationship. It was deeply repressed, and sublimated in the form of both men's intellectual speculation about the universal bisexuality of human beings.

4. See Alexander Grinstein, *On Sigmund Freud's Dreams* (Detroit: Wayne State University Press, 1968), 66.

5. For a recent definition of the "Isakower phenomenon" (adult hallucinations of the mother's breast) and the related "dream screen" and "blank dream" experiences, plus a valuable bibliography, see Philip M. Brombert, "On the Occurrence of the Isakower Phenomenon in a Schizoid Disorder," *Contemporary Psychoanalysis* 20, no. 4 (1984):600–601 and 623–24.

6. "From the History of an Infantile Neurosis" (1918), *SE* 17:7–122.

7. "Screen Memories" (1899), *SE* 3:303–22.

Notes

8. Siegfried Bernfeld, "An Unknown Autobiographical Fragment by Freud," *American Imago* 4, no. 1 (August 1946):3–19.

9. "The Archaic Features and Infantilism of Dreams," *Introductory Lectures*, no. 13, *SE* 15:199–212.

10. See also "Symbolism in Dreams," *Introductory Lectures*, no. 10, *SE* 15:155.

11. In a fine article supported by clinical examples, Owen Renik has recently tried to extend the concept of disguised reassurance in anxiety dreams. He claims that "similar disguised wish fulfillments can be identified in certain 'superego dreams' and in those post-traumatic dreams in which a traumatic event is accurately re-enacted." See "Typical Examination Dreams, 'Superego Dreams,' and Traumatic Dreams," *Psychoanalytic Quarterly* 50, no. 2 (1981):159.

12. As James Strachey points out in a footnote to this passage, Freud first clearly suggested the notion of the Oedipus complex in a letter to Fliess on 15 October 1897, although he was not to write the actual phrase *Oedipus complex* until 1910.

13. "A Short Account of Psycho-analysis" (1924), *SE* 19:208.

7. Why Dream? Wish Fulfillment versus Anxiety

1. For comments on Freud's strategies of presentation, see Hyman, *Tangled Bank*, 311–12. The starting point for Freud's concept of dreams as wish fulfillments was his observation of hallucinatory states in hospitalized psychotics, in whose delusions wish fulfillment often was obvious. In 1916 Freud issued an important clarification: "*what is unconscious in mental life is also what is infantile*. . . . If these evil impulses in dreams are merely infantile phenomena, a return to the beginnings of our ethical development (since dreams simply make us into children once more in our thoughts and feelings), we need not, if we are reasonable, be ashamed of these evil dreams" ("The Archaic Features and Infantilism of Dreams," *Introductory Lectures*, no. 13, *SE* 15:210–11).

2. Among modern psychoanalysts who emphasize dreams, Heinz Kohut is the most prominent one to claim that the successful analyst does not always need to identify unconscious infantile wishes and their distortion by the dream-work. See his *The Restoration of the Self* (New York: International Universities Press, 1977), 108–11.

3. "Children's Dreams," *Introductory Lectures*, no. 8, *SE* 15:129; cp. *Basic Psychoanalytic Concepts on the Theory of Dreams*, ed. Humberto Nagera et al. (London: Allen & Unwin, 1969), 22.

4. For a challenging commentary on Freud's concept of repression, see Samuel Weber, *The Legend of Freud* (Minneapolis: University of Minnesota Press, 1982), 42.

5. "Wish-Fulfilment," *Introductory Lectures*, no. 14, *SE* 15:217. After Freud had developed his theory of the ego, id, and superego, he modified his views on anxiety. He no longer defined it as a transformation of the original forbidden id-impulse as it passed through the preconscious on its way to consciousness, but rather as an anticipatory reaction by the ego against that impulse as it threatened to break through to consciousness. See "Inhibitions, Symptoms, and Anxiety," *SE* 20:109; cp. *Basic Psychoanalytic Concepts,* ed. Nagera, 107.

6. In 1924, with "The Economic Problem of Masochism," Freud changed his views (*SE* 19:155–70). He came to see masochism no longer as a secondary phenomenon derived from a primordial sadism, but rather as a primary manifestation of the "death-instinct." The original definition is more convincing. Today, the legitimacy of masochism as a diagnostic category is subject to intense debate since the concept can be abused by claiming that battered wives and rape victims unconsciously desire to be mistreated.

7. "Remarks on the Theory and Practice of Dream Interpretation," *SE* 19:118.

8. See also the extensive quotations in *Basic Psychoanalytic Concepts,* ed. Nagera, 108–10.

8. Dreams' Disguises

1. See *Jokes and Their Relation to the Unconscious* (1905) and *The Psychopathology of Everyday Life* (1901).

2. Freud discusses the process of dream formation more fully in "A Metapsychological Supplement to the Theory of Dreams" (1917), *SE* 14:225–29.

3. For Freud's shifting views on secondary elaboration see *Basic Psychoanalytic Concepts,* ed. Nagera, 62 and 88–92. Compare the influence of our desire for visual intelligibility in completing and rounding out what we see, as expounded for example by Rudolf Arnheim, *Art and Visual Perception: A Psychology of the Creative Eye. The New Version* (Berkeley and Los Angeles: University of California Press, 1974).

4. Gilbert D. Chaitin, "The Representation of Logical Relations in Dreams and the Nature of Primary Process," *Psychoanalysis and Contemporary Thought* 1 (1978):489. See also Stanley R. Palombo, "The Cognitive Act in Dream Construction," *Journal of the American Academy of Psychoanalysis* 8, no. 2 (April 1980):192–201.

Notes

5. See also the excellent discussion of the issue of interpretability in Weber, *Legend of Freud*, 65–83.

6. "The Dream-Work," *Introductory Lectures*, no. 11, *SE* 15:179–80.

7. *New Introductory Lectures*, *SE* 22:488–91.

8. "On Dreams," *SE* 5:651.

9. *Introductory Lectures*, *SE* 15:171.

10. "The Unconscious," *SE* 14:186.

11. *Introductory Lectures*, *SE* 15:174.

12. For detailed examples and interpretations of the dream-within-a-dream phenomenon, see Austin Silber, "A Significant 'Dream within a Dream,'" *Journal of the American Psychoanalytical Association* 31, no. 4 (1983):899–916; and Leon F. A. Berman, "Primal Scene Significance of a Dream within a Dream," *International Journal of Psychoanalysis* 66 (1985):75–76.

13. For Freud's repeated warnings on this point, see *Interpretation of Dreams*, 388–89 and 395; "On Dreams," *SE* 5:684; and "On Symbolism in Dreams," *Introductory Lectures*, no. 10, *SE* 15:151.

14. For background on studies of sexual symbolism before Freud, see Ellenberger, *Discovery*, 506–7.

15. *New Introductory Lectures*, *SE* 22:488–89.

16. "Character and Anal Eroticism," *SE* 9:174. Compare the common joking excuse, "the devil made me do it," an excuse that can become a horrifying reality to the psychotic.

17. "On Transformations of Instinct as Exemplified in Anal Eroticism" (1917), *SE* 17:131.

18. *New Introductory Lectures*, *SE* 22:488.

19. "From the History of an Infantile Neurosis" (1918), *SE* 17:107.

20. Another example: in his confessional autobiography *Si le grain ne meurt* (*If It Die . . .* , 1926), the French writer André Gide tells of being taken to his doctor's office as a child. He was shown a collection of sharp knives of all shapes and sizes on the wall that were supposedly to be used to punish him if he touched his penis again.

21. See also *New Introductory Lectures*, *SE* 22:488.

22. See Robert E. Scholes, *Semiotics and Interpretation* (New Haven, Conn.: Yale University Press, 1982).

23. See Brombert, "On the Occurrence of the Isakower Phenomenon"; Melanie Klein, "Envy and Gratitude," in *Envy and Gratitude and Other Works, 1946–63* (London: Hogarth, 1975), 176–235; and Harry Guntrip, *Schizoid Phenomena, Object-Relations, and the Self* (New York: International Universities Press, 1968).

24. Frank Patalano, "Color in Dreams and the Psychoanalytic Situation," *American Journal of Psychoanalysis* 44, no. 2 (Summer 1984):183–90.

9. "The Specimen Dream of Psychoanalysis"

1. "Sample" catches Freud's shade of meaning better than the generally accepted translation "specimen." Freud does not see this dream as something that has already been labeled, categorized, and exhaustively analyzed, but rather as something that he and the reader will begin to look at together as the first step in an adventure of self-discovery.

2. A translation of Artemidorus—coincidentally using the same title as Freud's work—has recently become available: *The Interpretation of Dreams*, trans. Robert J. White (Park Ridge, N.J.: Noyes Press, 1975).

3. In the original German, Irma and the dreamer address each other with the intimate *du* (thou) rather than the more formal *Sie* (you). Were they that close in real life or did Freud merely wish to be so? See Erik H. Erikson, "The Dream Specimen of Psychoanalysis," *Journal of the American Psychoanalytic Association* 2 (1954):24.

4. Frank R. Hartman, "A Reappraisal of the Emma Episode and the Specimen Dream," *Journal of the American Psychoanalytical Association* 31, no. 3 (1983):578–79. In the same passage Hartman quotes a 1908 letter to Abraham in which Freud admits to the fantasy of "sexual megalomania" hidden by the dream—having sex ("one simple therapy for widowhood") with all three unattached women in the dream.

5. "'Civilized Sexual Morality' and Modern Nervous Illness" (1908), *SE* 9:200.

6. Alan C. Elms, "Freud, Irma, Martha: Sex and Marriage and the 'Dream of Irma's Injection,'" *Psychoanalytic Review* 67 (1980):83–109.

7. Erikson, "Dream Specimen," 25–26, 41–42, and 54. In chronological order, other noteworthy detailed readings of the Irma dream include (1) Jacques Lacan, *Le Séminaire, Livre II. Le Moi dans la théorie de Freud et dans la technique de la psychanalyse*, chapters 13 and 14, pp. 177–204 (Paris: Seuil, 1978), summarized in English by William J. Richardson in *Interpreting Lacan*, ed. Joseph H. Smith and William Kerrigan (New Haven, Conn.: Yale University Press, 1983), 51–74. These lectures delivered in 1955 use the dream as a point of departure for discussing Freud's concept of the ego. (2) Didier Anzieu, *L'Auto-analyse* (Paris: Presses Universitaires de France, 1959), 29–39. He stresses Freud's fear of death suggested by the two young widows in the dream as "warnings of destiny" (Freud had had alarming heart symptoms the year before). (3) M. Schur, "Some Additional 'Day Residues' of 'The Specimen Dream of Psychoanalysis,'" *Psychoanalysis—A General Psychology,* ed. R. Lowenstein et al. (New York: International Universities Press, 1966), 45–

85. He sees the Irma dream as a disguised attempt to exculpate Freud's friend Fliess who had bungled a nose operation on a similar hysterical patient referred to him by Freud shortly before, nearly killing her. (4) Grinstein, *On Sigmund Freud's Dreams*, 23–46, and Swan, "*Mater* and Nannie," 34, see in the dream the reflection of "an aim-inhibited homosexual type of relationship" (Grinstein, 38) with Fliess. (5) Hartman, "Reappraisal of the Emma Episode." (6) Robert Langs, "Freud's Irma Dream and the Origins of Psychoanalysis," *Psychoanalytic Review* 71 (1984):591–617, stresses "Freud's effort to work over his anxieties and uncertainties regarding the psychoanalytic method, the conditions for psychoanalytic treatment, and the nature of the therapeutic relationship." He claims psychoanalysts have overlooked this dimension of the Irma dream because they are repressing their own deep conflicts regarding their profession (593). But intellectualizing and abstraction rob Langs's article of much of its potential force of conviction.

10. Dreams in Psychotherapy

1. Palombo, "Cognitive Act," 192–93.

2. "Remarks on the Theory and Practice of Dream-Interpretation" (1923), *SE* 19:109; on the technique of dream interpretation see also "The Manifest Content of Dreams and the Latent Dream-Thoughts," *Introductory Lectures*, no. 7, *SE* 15:113–25.

3. "On Dreams," *SE* 5:662; "The Dream-Work," *Introductory Lectures*, no. 11, *SE* 15:178.

4. For a recent approach that does base itself precisely on the continuity of the dream as story (the aesthetic approach), see Phillip McCaffrey, *Freud and Dora: The Artful Dream* (New Brunswick, N.J.: Rutgers University Press, 1984).

5. See R. E. Fancher and R. F. Strahan, "Galvanic Skin Response and the Secondary Revision of Dreams: A Partial Disconfirmation of Freud's Dream Theory," *Journal of Abnormal Psychology* 77 (1971):308–12.

6. For a rewarding, detailed discussion, see "Creative Writers and Day-Dreaming" (1908), *SE* 9:143–53.

7. "Resistance and Repression," *Introductory Lectures*, no. 19, *SE* 16:297.

8. "Some Neurotic Mechanisms in Jealousy, Paranoia and Homosexuality" (1922), *SE* 18:230. Near the end of his life, Freud recapitulated his views on dreams and madness in the first of the *New Introductory Lectures*, *SE* 22, chap. 29. Today, moreover, delusions themselves do not suffice to warrant a diagnosis of psychosis. Tumors, transient reactions to stress, and drugs may also cause them.

9. Patricia Carrington, "Dreams and Schizophrenia," *Archives of General Psychiatry* 26 (1972):343–50.

11. Conclusion: Challenges to Freud

1. Jung's muddy, confused style was an obstacle to his popularity until the 1964 publication of the lucid *Man and His Symbols* (Garden City, N.Y.: Doubleday) with its magnificent illustrations. His ideas, being much easier than Freud's to dramatize, have suggested the plots for a host of imaginative works ranging from Hermann Hesse's *Steppenwolf* to *Star Wars*.

2. Lacan's *The Four Fundamental Concepts of Psycho-Analysis* (London: Hogarth, 1977) repeatedly mentions the "Father, can't you see I'm burning?" dream (*Interpretation of Dreams*, 547–50, 571–72, et passim), but only briefly. (Lacan gave a full-scale reading of that dream, and also of the dream of the woman who had only smoked salmon for her dinner party, in his unpublished seminars during the 1950s). See also Jacques Derrida, "Freud and the Scene of Writing," and Jean Laplanche and Serge Leclaire, "The Unconscious: A Psychoanalytic Study," in *French Freud: Structural Studies in Psychoanalysis, Yale French Studies* 48 (1975):74–117, and 136–75, respectively.

3. See J. Allan Hobson and Robert W. McCarley, "The Brain as a Dream State Generator: An Activation-Synthesis Hypothesis of the Dream Process," *American Journal of Psychiatry* 134, no. 12 (December 1977):1335–48; and the refutation by Gerald W. Vogel, "An Alternative View of the Neurobiology of Dreaming," *American Journal of Psychiatry* 135, no. 12 (December 1978):1531–35.

4. David Foulkes, *Dreaming: A Cognitive-Psychological Analysis* (Hillsdale, N.J.: Lawrence Erlbaum, 1985), 95–107, 120–39; and *A Grammar of Dreams* (New York: Basic Books, 1978), chap. 4, especially 84–86, on unconscious wishes. Compare Freud's "Intellectual Activity in Dreams," chap. 6, in *The Interpretation of Dreams*, 481–96.

5. Some feminists, however, view this positively, seeing women's "amorality" as a source for an alternative to patriarchal superego morality. See *New Introductory Lectures, SE* 22:588, and "Female Sexuality" (1931), *SE* 21:225–43, on penis envy. On morality and sexuality see "Some Psychical Consequences of the Anatomical Distinction between the Sexes" (1925), *SE* 19:257–58.

6. "On Transformations of Instinct as Exemplified in Anal Eroticism" (1917), *SE* 17:127–33; "The Question of Lay Analysis" (1926), *SE* 20:212; "Analysis Terminable and Interminable" (1937), *SE* 23:209.

7. "Fragment of an Analysis of a Case of Hysteria," *SE* 7:60.

8. See Hannah S. Decker's clear-sighted "Freud and Dora: Constraints on Medical Progress," *Journal of Social History* 14 (1981):445–64.

Notes

9. See ibid. and also Madelon Sprengnether, "Enforcing Oedipus: Freud and Dora," in *In Dora's Case: Freud—Hysteria—Feminism*, ed. Charles Bernheimer and Claire Kahane (New York: Columbia University Press, 1985), 254–75. Her footnotes review the abundant earlier criticism well.

10. Jung, *Memories, Dreams, Reflections*, 158.

11. Recall the simpleminded furor that arose when former president Jimmy Carter confessed "I have committed adultery in my heart" during a *Playboy* interview.

12. Seymour Fisher and Roger P. Greenberg, *The Scientific Credibility of Freud's Theories and Therapy* (New York: Basic Books, 1977), 393–94.

13. Ibid., 5.

Bibliography

Primary Sources

The Interpretation of Dreams. Edited and translated by James Strachey. 1965. Reprint. New York: Avon Books, 1980. This inexpensive paperback contains the best English translation available at this date, plus an excellent introduction, index, and notes.

"Delusions and Dreams in Jensen's *Gradiva*" (1907). In *The Standard Edition of the Complete Psychological Works of Sigmund Freud*, edited and translated by James Strachey. 24 vols. London: Hogarth, 1953–74. Vol. 9, 7–95. An outstanding, pioneering application of dream analysis to literary criticism.

"Fragment of an Analysis of a Case of Hysteria" (1905). In *Standard Edition*, 7:7–122. The "Dora" (Ida Bauer) case, which Freud considered to be a sequel to *The Interpretation of Dreams*, and which illustrates for the first time the use of dreams in psychotherapy.

Introductory Lectures on Psycho-Analysis (1916–17). In *Standard Edition*, 15–16. Also published separately by W. W. Norton. Lectures 5–15 revise and update Freud's dream theory. Most noteworthy are lecture 10, a complete discussion of dream symbolism, and lecture 14, a lucid explanation of how Freud thinks dreams are formed. Of all his works, this one has probably been the most influential.

"On Dreams" (1901). In *Standard Edition*, 5:629–86. A simplified, greatly condensed version of *The Interpretation of Dreams*, published in 1901.

The Origins of Psycho-Analysis (Letters to Wilhelm Fliess, Drafts and Notes, 1887–1902). Edited by Marie Bonaparte, Anna Freud, and Ernst Kris. Garden City, N.Y.: Doubleday Anchor, 1957. Outstanding introduction and notes to this all-important document in the history of ideas, which reveals how Freud's thinking developed. *The Complete Letters of Sigmund Freud to Wilhelm Fliess, 1887–1904.* Edited and translated by Jeffrey Moussaieff Masson. Cambridge, Mass.: Harvard University Press,

Belknap Press, 1985, restores many omitted passages but is otherwise far less helpful.

"Remarks on the Theory and Practice of Dream Interpretation" (1922). In *Standard Edition*, 19:109–21. Supplements Freud's earlier views.

Nagera, Humberto, et al. *Basic Psychoanalytic Concepts on the Theory of Dreams*. London: Allen & Unwin, 1969. A useful compendium of Freud's remarks concerning dreams, arranged by topic with brief paraphrase and commentary.

Secondary Sources

Books

Bettleheim, Bruno. *Freud and Man's Soul*. 1982. Reprint. New York: Vintage Books, 1984. An eloquent, well-informed exposé of how English mistranslations have transformed Freud from a down-to-earth yet rather mystical thinker into an esoteric, scientistic technician.

Decker, Hannah S. *Freud in Germany: Revolution and Reaction in Science, 1893–1907*. Psychological Issues, no. 41. New York: International Universities Press, 1977. Chapter 10 treats dreams. Impeccable historical research situates Freud in the climate of scientific thought of his time.

Dement, William C. *Some Must Watch While Some Must Sleep*. New York: Simon & Schuster, 1976. The classic popularization of sleep research. Readable and enjoyable.

Ellenberger, Henri F. *The Discovery of the Unconscious: The History and Evolution of Dynamic Psychology*. New York: Basic Books, 1970. An important, monumental work that corrects Jones (see below) on many points and situates Freud broadly and masterfully in the history of ideas. Also treats rival psychoanalytic schools.

Fisher, Seymour, and Roger P. Greenberg. *The Scientific Credibility of Freud's Theories and Therapy*. New York: Basic Books, 1977. A balanced assessment based on many empirical studies.

Foulkes, David. *Dreaming: A Cognitive-Psychological Analysis*. Hillsdale, N.J. Lawrence Erlbaum, 1985. Influenced by Jean Piaget, Foulkes stresses that the ability to dream develops only gradually along with other mental capabilities. Authoritative; rich in ideas; highly recommended. The most serious recent challenge to Freud's ideas on dreams.

————. *A Grammar of Dreams*. New York: Basic Books, 1978. Chapter 4 evaluates Freudian dream theory carefully.

Grinstein, Alexander. *On Sigmund Freud's Dreams*. Detroit: Wayne State University Press, 1968. Studies nineteen dreams from *The Interpretation of Dreams* and from "On Dreams," describing the literary works and the lived experiences that Freud associated with them, and speculating in an orthodox Freudian manner on the psychoanalytical significance of areas not fully discussed by Freud—notably, infantile sexuality. Somewhat plodding, but valuable.

————. *Freud's Rules of Dream Interpretation*. Madison, Conn.: International Universities Press, 1983. A conscientious summary.

Hartmann, Ernest. *The Nightmare: The Psychology and Biology of Terrifying Dreams*. New York: Basic Books, 1984. The latest biochemical and psychological information on the various types of dreams. Supersedes Ernest Jones's landmark 1931 study.

Hyman, Stanley Edgar. *The Tangled Bank: Darwin, Marx, Frazer and Freud as Imaginative Writers*. New York: Atheneum, 1962. Excellent, original study. The authoritative conclusion places Freud in the context of modern thought.

Jones, Ernest. *The Life and Work of Sigmund Freud*. 3 vols. New York: Basic Books, 1953–57. The unrivaled biography by Freud's lifelong friend and associate. Contains some major errors based on Freud's own statements. Abridged into one volume by Lionel Trilling and Steven Marcus in 1961.

Laplanche, Jean. *The Language of Psychoanalysis*. New York: Norton, 1973. This valuable reference work explains key psychoanalytic terminology, translations of which are provided in several languages. Useful excerpts are provided in *Yale French Studies* 48 (1972):179–202.

Mayes, Andrew Richard, ed. *Sleep Mechanisms and Functions in Humans and Animals: An Evolutionary Perspective*. Wokingham, Berkshire, England: Van Nostrand Reinhold, 1983. How human sleep and dreaming compares with that of other species; see the introduction and chapters 5, 9–12.

McCaffrey, Phillip. *Freud and Dora: The Artful Dream*. New Brunswick, N.J.: Rutgers University Press, 1984. An "aesthetic" approach tries to interpret Dora's dreams as if they were works of literature. Debatable but intelligent.

Porter, Laurence M. "Dreams Real and Literary." In *The Literary Dream in French Romanticism: A Psychoanalytic Interpretation*, 1–12. Detroit: Wayne State University Press, 1979. Discusses the difficulties involved in trying to deal with literary dreams as if they were the dreams of a client in therapy.

Bibliography

Van DeCastle, Robert L. *The Psychology of Dreaming*. Morristown, N.J.: General Learning Press, 1971. An excellent brief history of theories about dreams, 11–21, and a lucid method of content analysis, 34–37.

Woods, Ralph L., and Herbert B. Greenhouse, eds. *The New World of Dreams*. New York: Macmillan, 1974. A rich, varied, well-selected and skillfully edited collection of brief articles and excerpts on research in dream theory.

Articles

Carrington, Patricia. "Dreams and Schizophrenia." *Archives of General Psychiatry* 16 (1972):343–50. "In general the schizophrenic dreams gave the impression of an acute state of emergency or stress, while the control dreams depicted everyday, practical concerns."

Decker, Hannah S. "Freud and Dora: Constraints on Medical Progress." *Journal of Social History* 14 (1981):445–64. A balanced assessment. Women dissatisfied with marriage and motherhood could find no other outlet at the time, nor could Freud have done better given the state of psychiatric knowledge around 1900.

Elms, Alan C. "Freud, Irma, Martha: Sex and Marriage and the 'Dream of Irma's Injection.'" *Psychoanalytic Review* 67 (1980):83–109. How Freud's sexual frustrations in his marriage may be reflected in this dream; a thorough, careful treatment.

Erikson, Erik H. "The Dream Specimen of Psychoanalysis." *Journal of the American Psychoanalytic Association* 2 (1954):5–56. Centers on the Irma dream. A masterful development of Freud's theories of dream interpretation, specifying what to look for in clinical practice. The most famous of all articles on dreams.

Gilligan, Carol. "The Conquistador and the Dark Continent: Reflections on the Psychology of Love." *Daedalus* 113 (Summer 1984):75–95. A lucid, accessible article on the shortcomings of Freud's theories as they relate to women; traces the development of his thought quite well.

Kermode, Frank. "Freud and Interpretation." *International Review of Psycho-Analysis* 12, no. 1 (1985):3–12. A clear, wide-ranging discussion of the crucial issue of what "interpretation" means.

Reis, Walter J. "A Comparison of the Interpretation of Dream Series with and without Free Associations." In *Dreams and Personality Dynamics*, edited by Manfred F. DeMartino, 211–25. Springfield, Ill.: Charles C. Thomas, 1959. Given about twenty-five dreams or more, psychologists make the same assessments of the dreamer's personality whether or not they can also see the dreamer's associations to the dreams.

Renik, Owen. "Typical Examination Dreams, 'Superego Dreams,' and Traumatic Dreams." *Psychoanalytic Quarterly* 50, no. 2 (1981):159–89. A fine, convincing article claims that dreams of a danger one has escaped serve to reassure the dreamer.

Silverstein, Barry. "Freud's Psychology and Its Organic Foundation: Sexuality and Mind-Body Interactionism." *Psychoanalytic Review* 72, no. 2 (Summer 1985):203–28. A cogent recent view of the relationship between body and mind.

Sprengnether, Madelon. "Enforcing Oedipus: Freud and Dora." In *In Dora's Case: Freud—Hysteria—Feminism,* edited by Charles Bernheimer and Claire Kahane, 254–75. New York: Columbia University Press, 1985. The best article in the volume. Claims Freud writes the case history to exact revenge from "Dora." The footnotes provide a lucid review of much earlier criticism of this case history.

Stein, Martin H. "Rational versus Anagogic Interpretation: Xenophon's Dream and Others." *Journal of the American Psychoanalytical Association* 32, no. 3 (1984):529–56. Excellent study of two traditions of dream interpretation.

Swan, Jim. "*Mater* and Nannie: Freud's Two Mothers and the Discovery of the Oedipus Complex." *American Imago* 31 (1974):1–64. How Freud's remembered sexual feelings for his mother and his nurse influenced his self-discovery.

Bibliographies

Grinstein, Alexander. *Sigmund Freud's Writings: A Comprehensive Bibliography.* New York: International Universities Press, 1977.

Psychological Abstracts. Lancaster, Pa.: American Psychological Association, 1927–. Monthly with quarterly cumulations. International scope. The very prompt coverage runs from six months to one year behind publication. See headings "Dream Analysis" and "Dream Content."

University of California at Los Angeles. Brain Information Service. Sleep Research Institute. *Sleep Research Abstracts,* 1972–. Annual.

Index

Index

About the Author

Laurence M. Porter received three degrees from Harvard University and also studied at the Sorbonne. He has taught French and Comparative Literature at Michigan State University since 1963. In 1980 he served as Andrew W. Mellon Distinguished Visiting Professor of Comparative Literature at the University of Pittsburgh. He is an active member of the Michigan Society for Psychoanalytic Psychology, and the author of two books including *The Literary Dream in French Romanticism: A Psychoanalytical Approach* (Wayne State University Press, 1979). He has also edited *Critical Essays on Gustave Flaubert* (G. K. Hall, 1986) and with the psychotherapist Laurel Porter, co-edited *Aging in Literature* (1984). He has published sixty articles and book chapters in six countries, in such journals as the *American Imago, Comparative Literature Studies*, the *Journal of Aesthetics and Art Criticism*, the *Journal of Altered States of Consciousness, Oeuvres et Critiques*, the *Romanic Review, Studies in Romanticism*, and *Symposium*. He serves on the editorial boards of *Nineteenth-Century French Studies* and of the international scholarly journal *Degré Second*.